Catholic and Evangelical Praise for
Mary, Mother of the Son

Mark Shea has written the single most helpful book on Sacred Tradition written in our generation. In other books he has illumined the reading of Scripture and the worship of the Eucharist. Now, in *Mary, Mother of the Son*, he takes us to the summit of creation, the Ark of the New Covenant, the true tabernacle of the Lord. To read this book is to love Christ as a brother, by honoring the mother he shares with us (John 19:27).

> — SCOTT HAHN, PH.D.,
> Professor of Scripture and Theology, Franciscan
> University of Steubenville; Author, *Hail, Holy Queen*

I recommend that Evangelicals read *Mary, Mother of the Son*. They will certainly find much here to challenge and disagree with, but they will also find a Catholic perspective on Mary that takes into account evangelical concerns. Mark Shea's honest depiction of his own Marian pilgrimage contributes to greater mutual understanding about the wonderful handmaiden of the Lord whom all Christians in all generations call "blessed."

> — DR. TIMOTHY GEORGE,
> Dean, Beeson Divinity School, Samford University

With wit, wisdom, theological weight, and a whole lot of style Mark Shea delivers a work that helps readers plunge into the mystery and beauty of the Mother of *the* Son, the Blessed Virgin Mary. Catholics and non-Catholics alike will gain much from this well-developed trilogy and may well find themselves falling in love with the Virgin of Nazareth whose *fiat* birthed salvation to the world. I am eager to share *Mary, Mother of the Son* with everyone I know!

> — JOHNNETTE S. BENKOVIC
> Founder and President: Women of Grace®,
> Living His Life Abundantly®
> Host of *The Abundant Life* seen internationally on
> EWTN and Women of Grace Live Radio

This fine book exploring the Church's teaching on Our Lady will be a joy to Catholics and a revelation to Protestants. I highly recommend it for both groups.

— FATHER BENEDICT J. GROESCHEL, C.F.R.

Mary, Mother of the Son is a winsome book. This is not to say his arguments are not rigorous and carefully thought through. They are. Rather, it is a winsome book in that it is invitational. Mark Shea is a gracious host inviting others to explore with him the marvels of the wondrous place he now calls home, the Catholic Church.

— RICHARD JOHN NEUHAUS
Editor-in-Chief, *First Things*

Mark Shea's *Mary, Mother of the Son* is a comprehensive and engaging treatment of the Church's teaching on Mary. A skilled writer, he renders complexities with simplicity without diluting them in the least. His own past experience as an Evangelical Christian and now Catholic enable him to offer helpful and thorough answers to the most common—and uncommon—questions readers from any background might have about Mary.

— AMY WELBORN
Author, *Mary and the Christian Life*

Recent years have seen a rapprochement between Catholics and Evangelicals, a large part of which has involved renewed Evangelical interest in the figure of Mary. One thinks in particular of Tim Perry's *Mary for Evangelicals* or Scot McKnight's *The Real Mary*. Evangelicals (as well as others) who would like to learn more about the role Mary plays in traditional Roman Catholic faith and practice now have at their disposal Mark Shea's wonderful tripartite work, *Mary, Mother of the Son*. Shea's clear, lucid, learned and often witty writing on the rich subject of Mariology is a pleasure to digest.

— DR. LEROY HUIZENGA
Assistant Professor of New Testament, Wheaton College

In his winsome, witty style, Mark Shea winds his way through the many rooms of Marian doctrines that separate the Roman Catholic faithful from the Protestant believer who thinks each and every doctrine must be fully supported by the Bible. I suspect curious evangelicals and skeptical Catholics will find much to think about in *Mary, Mother of the Son*.

> — SCOT MCKNIGHT, Karl A. Olsson Professor in Religious Studies, North Park University
> Author, *The Real Mary*

Mark Shea did not lose any of his Evangelical zeal when he found his home in the Roman Catholic Church. In *Mary, Mother of the Son*, he challenges many Evangelical worries about Mary and explains both dogmatic and discretionary Marian beliefs and practices simply, clearly, and sometimes wittily. Evangelical Protestants will leave this book with a better understanding of why so many Christians find devotion to Mary to help rather than hinder devotion to her Son.

> — TIM PERRY, Associate Professor of Theology,
> Providence College, Otterburne, Manitoba, Canada
> Author, *Mary for Evangelicals: Toward an Understanding of the Mother of Our Lord*

I've been challenged to open my heart and my mind to the complexities of a love-relationship with the mother of Jesus and her living legacy. . . . I would now probably even go so far as to say her living "presence" among us. Shea is an astoundingly gifted writer; communicating with ease, depth, humor, warmth and genuine love for your readers. I applaud this amazing work of brilliance, insight, devotion and faith. "Well done, O good and faithful servant."

> — THE REV. DR. DOUGLAS E. MILLHAM
> President, Discover the World, Inc.

Mary, Mother of the Son I:
Modern Myths and Ancient Truth

MARK P. SHEA

Mary, Mother of the Son
Volume One:

Modern Myths and Ancient Truth

CATHOLIC
ANSWERS

SAN DIEGO
2009

Published by Catholic Answers, Inc.
2020 Gillespie Way
El Cajon, California 92020
(888) 291-8000 (orders)
(619) 387-0042 (fax)
www.catholic.com (web)

Cover design by Devin Schadt
Typesetting by Loyola Book Composition

Printed in the United States of America
ISBN 978-1933919-19-5

To Pope John Paul the Great,
who showed the world
that a heart consecrated to Mary
is a heart consecrated to Jesus Christ.

And to my Mother in Christ,
the Blessed Virgin Mary:

Totus Tuus

Acknowledgments

Thanks above all to God, the Father, Son and Holy Spirit, from whom, to whom and through whom this book and all things exist. Blessed be he!

Thanks also to Janet, my wife, for showing me both Mary and Jesus in the beauty of her being. Also, to our boys, Luke, Matthew, Peter, and Sean, of whom I am so proud. I love you all. Singers, Comics, Dreamers, and Discoverers are all enriched by God's calling you into being and redeeming you. I'm glad you are and I thank God for you all!

In addition, heaps o'thanks go to:

Karl Keating, Jimmy Akin, and the fine folk at Catholic Answers.

Tom Allen, president of CatholicExchange.com for rooting for this book. Not to mention the whole gang at CE! Thanks for making it possible, guys!

Sherry Curp, Ian McLean, and Dean Tudor, whose editorial acumen made the book more chewy, less cakey, and much tastier.

Fr. Brian Stanley and the good folk of St. Charles Borromeo parish in Coldwater, Michigan, who prayed this book into being.

Fr. Richard John Neuhaus, for his kind interest in and support of this project.

Sandra Miesel, Carl Olsen, Amy Welborn, Ted Sri and various other crack troops in the war on *Da Vinci Code*-inspired doltishness.

Dr. Scott Hahn, who pointed me to several valuable resources as I researched the book.

My dear friend Sherry Weddell and the gang at the Catherine of Siena Institute in Colorado Springs, Colorado. You guys do awesome work!

Dale Ahlquist, president of the G. K. Chesterton Society, for being such a thoughtful and funny guy—like Chesterton, only thinner.

G. K. Chesterton, who is not just Dale's hero, but mine as well.

Fr. Michael Sweeney, O.P., from whom I have stolen many brilliant ideas.

Dave Curp. Historian Extraordinaire and Beloved Brother, from whom I have stolen the rest of my brilliant ideas.

Michael Lounsbery, who gave me the hilarious list!

C. S. Lewis, yet another of my heroes.

Steve Ray, with profound gratitude for your enthusiastic support!

Donal Foley of Theotokos Books in the U.K. (http://theotokos .org.uk). Thanks for the apparitions info in the Appendix for *Volume Three: Miracles, Devotion, and Motherhood*! I owe you one!

Bob Halligan, Jr., and the merry rock and rollers who constitute Ceili Rain. No you, no great quote for Chapter 6! Thanks for the blessing of your music. Bishop Ross Owen Davies and the priests of the Anglican Diocese of the Murray, Australia, fellow seekers in the Great Regathering.

J. S. Bach, The Montreux Band, Darol Anger, Mike Marshall, Pat Metheny, Phil Keaggy, Nightnoise, Duke Ellington, They Might Be Giants: musicians whose beauty helped me write.

Homestarrunner.com, for giving me something to laugh at during break time.

Jon Sorensen, Air Traffic Controller and amazingly patient guy!

Jane Cavolina, copy editor extraordinaire!

John O'Rourke, greatest typesetter in America!

Caroline Manno, proofreader par excellence.

The incredibly patient readers of *Catholic and Enjoying It!* Thanks for putting up with my long absence. Just in case you forgot the URL during the long book-writing hiatus, it's still http://markshea.blogspot.com.

The people of Blessed Sacrament parish in Seattle, Washington. Thanks for being our home until we reach our long home.

Also, special thanks to Saints Jerome, Athanasius, Anthony of the Desert, Francis de Sales, Dominic, Tertius, and, of course, Mama Mary, on whose constant intercession I rely for help. *Ora pro nobis*.

Contents

Foreword

If I said that Mark Shea is an apologist, many of our contemporaries might respond, "Why? What did he do wrong?"

As the readers of this book undoubtedly know, to be an apologist does not mean one is apologizing for having done something wrong. The Latin *apologia* does not mean an apology in the usual sense of that word. It means a defense of what one believes to be true.

In recent decades, the genre of Christian thinking and writing that is called apologetics fell on hard times. All kinds of reasons contributed to this, but they need not delay us here. It is not as though apologetics is not firmly grounded in the Church's history and mission. We read in the New Testament, "Always be prepared to make a defense to any one who calls you to account for the hope that is in you, yet do it with gentleness and reverence" (1 Pet. 3:15).

Mark Shea is prepared to make a defense, and he does it with gentleness and reverence. And with a great deal of wit and charm. *Mary, Mother of the Son* is a winsome book. This is not to say that his arguments are not rigorous and carefully thought through. They are. Rather, it is a winsome book in that it is invitational. Mark Shea is a gracious host inviting others to explore with him the marvels of the wondrous place he now calls home, the Catholic Church.

He once viewed this home from a distance, and with considerable suspicion, indeed hostility. And then everything changed. Not all at once, mind you. It took a lot of prayer and study and argument before he realized that one of the chief reasons for his suspicion and hostility was turning into an object of love. To put it simply, Mark Shea fell in love with Mary and, as is the way with lovers, he wants to tell us all about it.

Listening to a lover talk about his beloved can be, quite frankly, something of a bore. That is most decidedly not the case with this book. The author's discoveries and resulting devotion are contagious. Perhaps the book should carry a warning label to that effect.

Mark Shea was an Evangelical Protestant, and his writing reflects an Evangelical earnestness about the question, "What does the Bible say?" What he discovered is that the Bible says ever so much more, and not only about Mary, when it is read in the light of centuries of Christian reflection on what the Bible says. The author understands that, in becoming a Catholic, he became more fully the Christian he was as an Evangelical.

Of course, Catholics, especially cradle Catholics, might be inclined to think that what Mark Shea has discovered they knew all along, and therefore there is not much point in them reading this book. That is far from the truth.

Catholics need to read this book. Because it will help them respond to non-Catholics who are puzzled about our devotion to Mary. And, at least equally important, because it will introduce them to the treasury of scriptural and traditional wisdom about Mary who is the Mother of God—which means that she is the mother of Jesus Christ who is true God and true man.

As Mark Shea understands, all Mariology (teaching about Mary) is really Christology (teaching about Christ). In drawing closer to Mary, we are drawn closer to Christ; in drawing closer to Christ, we are drawn closer to Mary. Why that is the case is the subject of this delightful and informative book.

Fr. Richard John Neuhaus[1]
Requiescat in pace, 2009

---

[1] Father Richard John Neuhaus was a priest of the archdiocese of New York, the editor-in-chief of *First Things*, and the author of many books, including *Catholic Matters: Confusion, Controversy, and the Splendor of Truth* (Basic Books).

Introduction: The Quest Continues

Now this is not the end. It is not even the beginning of the end. But it is, perhaps, the end of the beginning.

—Winston Churchill

"Darling, I know you were raised Catholic and I know you don't see the harm in it, but I'm asking you to please stop praying to Mary. It's not in Scripture and I think it's spiritually dangerous."

I said those words to my wife, Janet, in 1984, a few months after we were married. To me, as an Evangelical, Marian devotion appeared to be indistinguishable from the occult attempt to summon the dead. Would a Christian go to a medium and ask her to talk to the spirit of his dead grandmother for advice on handling the kids? Should a Christian consult a horoscope instead of God because it's consoling? Jan's prayers to Mary and the saints genuinely worried me, particularly since Scripture seemed to plainly condemn it:

> And when they say to you, "Consult the mediums and the wizards who chirp and mutter," should not a people consult their God? Should they consult the dead on behalf of the living? To the teaching and to the testimony! Surely for this word which they speak there is no dawn. They will pass through the land, greatly distressed and hungry; and when they are hungry, they will be enraged and will curse their king and their God, and turn their faces upward; and they will look to the earth, but behold, distress and darkness, the gloom of anguish; and they will be thrust into thick darkness (Is. 8:19–22).

Marian devotion, like the rest of the so-called "cult of the saints" appeared to me (as it does to millions of Evangelicals) to be a huge distraction from the worship of the Holy One, an immense detour around his very clear commandment: "I am the LORD your God, who brought you out of the land of Egypt, out of the house of bondage. You shall have no other gods before me" (Ex. 20:2–3).

Moreover, it seemed to me that, even for Catholics who did not have a particularly strong tendency to pray to Mary, there was still the problem that the official Catholic Church had freighted the gospel with a great deal of extra junk about her. There was the unbiblical title "Mother of God"—as though the Ancient of Days could have a mother! There were the official dogmas of Mary's Perpetual Virginity, Immaculate Conception, and Assumption into Heaven. All this was supposed to be an "infallible" part of the Catholic faith. But wasn't all that stuff just borrowing from paganism and adding to the word of God?

In addition, there was the problem of things which, while not exactly dogma, were not particularly discouraged in the Church either. With Catholics, it seemed like everywhere you turned, Mary popped out at you from holy cards, Rosaries, little shrines, garish statues, and all sorts of bric-a-brac. Catholics liked to sing hymns of praise to Mary and to call her "Queen of Heaven." Didn't they realize the "Queen of Heaven" was a pagan goddess condemned by the prophet Jeremiah (cf. Jer. 7:18)? Some Catholics even talked about Mary being a "Co-Redemptrix," despite Scripture clearly stating, "[T]here is one mediator between God and men, the man Christ Jesus" (1 Tim. 2:5). And what was the story with all those "apparitions" anyway? Every couple of months I'd open the paper and read about Mary showing up in a water stain on a parish wall, or in a reflection cast by a window. Why was this sort of thing considered more credible than Oral Roberts claiming to see a nine-hundred-foot tall Jesus demanding cash?

So my general impression of Marian teaching and devotion was not what you would call warm and affirming. Yes, I knew there were (as I would have said at that time) "Catholics who are also Christian." But it seemed to me that, on the whole, pretty much the entirety of Catholic Marian teaching and devotion was a vast mass of pagan barnacles encrusted on the hull of the R.M.S.

Catholic Church after two thousand years of sailing through the waters of history. The Catholic Church, it seemed to me, would be far better off if some pope or council would scour off all that Mary junk and get back to the simplicity of the biblical gospel. Yes, there were those few Catholics (like my wife, Pope John Paul II, Mother Teresa, St. Augustine, St. Thomas, G. K. Chesterton, Peter Kreeft, St. Francis and . . . hmmmm . . . well, maybe more than just a few . . .) who had a profound devotion to Mary and had not forgotten their relationship with Christ. Indeed, oddly, these people seemed to have a stronger relationship with Christ than I did. But still, I told myself, that was only because of divine grace mercifully protecting them from fully living out the idolatry inherent in their ignorant beliefs. God must not be tempted, and there was no reason to count on him protecting everybody who remained ignorant of the true gospel. The norm, I assumed, was that Marian devotion was a slippery slope that would, apart from God's inscrutable protection of certain blessed individuals, lead inexorably toward worshipping the creature instead of the Creator. It was, I thought, a classic example of what happens when people trust Tradition and not Scripture.

Readers of my book *By What Authority?: An Evangelical Discovers Catholic Tradition* know how I came to change very profoundly that view of sacred Tradition. I discovered it is not true that Catholics rely on sacred Tradition and Evangelicals don't. Rather, Catholics rely on sacred Tradition and know they do, while Evangelicals rely on sacred Tradition and typically don't know they do. Consequently, I was faced with a challenge. According to Catholic belief, the very doctrines that irk most Protestant believers (including the Marian doctrines) are those that cannot be set aside, since they are as much a part of apostolic teaching as the deity of Christ. The very same apostolic authority that tells us what is and is not in our Bible speaks in a coherent voice of authority through a line of bishops leading back to Jesus Christ himself and says it is vital to acknowledge that the ever-virgin Mary is the Mother of God who was immaculately conceived and assumed into Heaven.

In short, I was obliged either to:

1. Find out if the whole Catholic Tradition was truly coherent; or,

2. Reject arbitrarily the bits I was uncomfortable with, but simultaneously exploit Catholic Tradition's authority where it was useful against modernism—all the while hoping that both Evangelicals and modernists (not to mention the Holy Spirit) would not laugh at my wholesale inconsistency.[1]

So in discovering the reality of sacred Tradition, I had not reached the end of my journey. I had not even reached the beginning of the end. But I had, perhaps, reached the end of the beginning. I had not finished exploring the Catholic faith by a long shot. Rather, I was simply given a sense of how big it really was. I was no longer in a position automatically to conflate an extra-biblical teaching with an anti-biblical one. Now I had to discover whether any Catholic teachings were actually anti-biblical—including the Marian doctrines.

By the time I entered the Church, I was persuaded that there were no anti-biblical Catholic teachings—not even the Marian ones. But this doesn't mean that I completely understood all things Marian at that point. Jesus' grace provided sufficient softening and seeding of the ground so that I didn't find Marian devotion and doctrine impossible to accept upon my entry into the Church. But although I had come to the conclusion that there was nothing anti-biblical in the Marian doctrines, I still didn't get Mary. I knew what Catholic teaching wasn't: it wasn't anti-biblical. But I didn't know what it was. Catholic Marian devotion didn't appeal to me and, in many cases, it still gave me the willies well after I became Catholic. So, curiously, most of the actual "discovery" of Mary took place after I became Catholic, not before.

Some folks find this hard to understand. After all, when you enter the Catholic Church, you're required to say, "I believe and

---

[1] Mark P. Shea, *By What Authority?: An Evangelical Discovers Catholic Tradition* (Huntington, Ind.: Our Sunday Visitor, 1996), 174–75.

profess all that the Holy Catholic Church believes, teaches and proclaims to be revealed by God."[2] How could I say that if I didn't even understand most of the stuff about Mary and was still rather edgy about large portions of it?

That question reminds me of the joke about the Marxist who heard a proposal for a very sensible economic program that conflicted with his diagram of the universe. "Oh sure, it will work in reality," he replied, "but will it work in theory?" Theoretically (according to some people), every Catholic convert has worked through every conceivable permutation of Catholic theology before he enters the Church, and anything less is a half-baked conversion. In reality, however, experience from the New Testament onward shows that people can know enough to become Catholic while still having many questions that need to be answered later.

The disciples live this paradox when they struggle with some of Jesus' hard sayings, such as his disturbing remark that "unless you eat the flesh of the Son of man and drink his blood, you have no life in you" (John 6:53). Jesus, up until that point, had had a substantial entourage of disciples and hangers-on who—what with interesting preaching, free food, the occasional miracle, and the pleasure of watching Jesus unsettle some disliked authority figures—had carved out a comfy little groove for themselves in the company of the latest counterculture figure.

But now the teacher was starting to sound weird. "Eat his flesh? Drink his blood? He's starting to lose it," most of them said. Result: Many of his disciples bailed. John records, "After this many of his disciples drew back and no longer went about with him" (John 6:66). Jesus was creeping out his disciples.

However, Jesus wasn't in a hurry to regain the entourage. Instead, he challenged the disciples who remained, saying, "Do you also wish to go away?" (John 6:67). Simon Peter's answer was not, "I refuse to follow you another step until you put a written

---

[2] *The Rites of the Catholic Church*, vol. 1 (Collegeville, Minn.: Liturgical Press, 1990), 280.

explanation of this outrageous behavior on my desk. I'm not some dumb sheep, you know! I am a Thinking Adult who deserves to have my concerns addressed and who does not appreciate all this stuff about 'trusting' and 'mystery.'" Instead, Simon Peter answered him as many a Catholic convert has replied when faced with one of the many mysteries of this strange divine sea of a faith:

> Lord, to whom shall we go? You have the words of eternal life; and we have believed, and have come to know, that you are the Holy One of God (John 6:68–69).

It is interesting that, so far as we can tell from Scripture, Jesus didn't reply to Simon Peter's offering of faith with a cross-referenced treatise on the Eucharist. Instead, he chose to let the disciples muddle along with no explanation of what this mysterious saying was all about. And when Jesus finally did return to the subject of the Eucharist, he more or less explained his mysterious words in John 6 with even more mysterious words at the Last Supper. For Jesus' strange commands, "Take, eat; this is my body" and "Drink of it, all of you; for this is my blood of the covenant, which is poured out for many for the forgiveness of sins" (Matt. 26:26–28), are given without explanation to a gaggle of disciples who likely no more understood this than they understood his explicit prophecy that "he must go to Jerusalem and suffer many things from the elders and chief priests and scribes, and be killed, and on the third day be raised" (Matt. 16:21). In short, they believed, but they did not understand. Indeed, they believed in order to understand.

The first disciples of the apostles did likewise: They knew enough to come to faith, but there was still a lot they didn't know. The apostles received them in their infant faith, but did not leave them as infants. The author of Hebrews writes: "You need milk, not solid food; for every one who lives on milk is unskilled in the word of righteousness, for he is a child. But solid food is for the mature" (Heb. 5:12–14). Note that he does not chide his readers for converting while they were still on a milk diet. Rather, he chides them for staying on a milk diet. He assumes, as a normal part of the Christian life, that converts will come to understand things after conversion that they did not understand at Baptism. He does not say, "If you didn't understand this before, you should have waited till you did before converting."

For this reason, Catholic teaching has historically been divided between catechesis and mystagogia. Catechesis is the introduction to the mysteries of the faith in preparation for receiving the sacraments of Baptism, Confirmation and the Eucharist at Easter. Through it, those approaching Baptism learn the basic shape of the Church's faith (outlined in the Nicene Creed and prayed aloud by Catholic worshippers during the Mass). Instruction is also given about the meaning and importance of the seven sacraments instituted by our Lord, as well as the Church's moral teaching (summarized in the Ten Commandments and the Beatitudes). Finally, catechumens are introduced to the interior life through study of the Our Father (also known as the Lord's Prayer). Not all Catholics get even this much instruction: St. Philip baptized the Ethiopian eunuch on the day they met (cf. Acts 8:26–39). But the whole point of catechesis is to give a person enough information to assent intelligently to the saving lordship of Jesus Christ and to understand what he is promising to do when he enters the Catholic Church.

Catechesis is like a map. A good study of a map of my hometown, Seattle, will give you the general lay of the land. But reading a map of Seattle isn't the same as living there and getting to know all the amazing things Seattle has to offer. The map won't tell you about that little cafe in Fremont, or the great little playground in the U District, or that pizza place in Belltown that makes the best cappuccino in the city. It's the same deal with catechesis. Entering the Church with a basic knowledge of her teaching is not the same as living in the Church and plumbing her depths to make the innumerable connections with the "riches of his glorious inheritance in the saints" (Eph. 1:18) God wishes us to make. For that, the new Catholic may need a little help. Thus, second course of instruction and reflection after entry into the Church is provided by mystagogia.

Now as it happened, my early years as a Catholic had no formal mystagogia. However, the Holy Spirit, in his kindness, put me in contact with plenty of resources and good people who, in one way or another, helped me undergo a sort of impromptu mystagogia. This is not to claim I had any special mystical insight. Indeed, with rare exceptions, there was nothing more mystical about the things I learned than the sort of everyday mysticism all Catholics enjoy simply by being Catholic and participating in the great mysteries known as sacraments. I certainly experienced no Marian apparitions. Nope, what I learned was how to go out and find information for myself instead of waiting around for somebody to hand it to me.

The information is, in fact, readily available. It's right there in Scripture, the *Catechism of the Catholic Church*, the writings of the Church Fathers, the teaching of the councils and the popes, and plenty of easy-to-read books and easy-to-understand materials produced by a growing battalion of Catholic writers and teachers (included in a handy bibliography at the end of this book).

And what did I find as I went out and discovered what the Church says, believes, feels, thinks and does about the Blessed Virgin Mary? That, my friends, is the subject of the *Mary, The Mother of the Son* trilogy. These are the books I wished someone had written when I was coming into the Church. They are designed to address the numerous questions that Marian doctrine and devotion arouses, not simply among Evangelical converts like me, but even among many Catholics and non-Christians.

The first volume—*Modern Myths and Ancient Truth*—deals with the fundamental question of where the Church gets its teaching about Mary. This is crucial, since misunderstandings and falsehoods abound. Many people are convinced that Marian doctrine and devotion is nothing more than repackaged pagan mythology that has little or nothing to do with the teaching of the apostles.

Modern Myths and Ancient Truth demonstrates the falseness of this notion, and shows that the Church's teaching concerning Mary is, indeed, apostolic and profoundly biblical. We discover the strange paradox of how the gospel of grace crowns and perfects not only the Old Testament, but the deepest insights of the great non-Christian philosophies, religions, and myths. We learn how to read the Bible as the earliest Christians did and find that Mary, far from distracting us from her son, refers us to him and protects the deepest truths about him and his Church.

The second volume—*First Guardian of the Truth*—addresses the Church's four essential teachings about the Blessed Virgin. In this volume, we learn what these teachings are (and are not), discover their roots in apostolic revelation, and discuss why they are essential for a healthy understanding of Christ and his Church. We also discover the astonishing relevance each of these teachings has, not only for the Christian believer, but for the twenty-first-century world as it comes to grips with questions concerning the dignity, origin, and destiny of the human person.

Finally, the third volume—*Miracles, Devotion, and Motherhood*—looks at the place of Mary and the saints in the devotional life of the Church. If *First Guardian of the Truth* is about what must be believed about Mary, this volume is about what may be believed about Mary. It discusses the communion of saints, the Holy Rosary, other Marian devotions and titles, the phenomenon of private revelation (such as Marian apparitions), and, finally, some of the ways that our Lady is being rediscovered in the Church and in the world.

Mary is, without comparison, the single most significant woman who ever lived. If you are among the millions who regard her as intriguing, frightening, a source of peace, a source of conflict, a puzzle, a distraction, a vision of holiness, a great big nothing, an idol, or a radiant splendor, please do join my rediscovery of this most consequential of women. You may be in for some surprises: I know I certainly was. And I know that I'm glad—very glad—to have been surprised.

I

Pseudo-Knowledge from Venus and Mars

The modern world will accept no dogmas upon any authority; but it will accept any dogmas on no authority. Say that a thing is so, according to the Pope or the Bible, and it will be dismissed as a superstition without examination. But preface your remark merely with "they say" or "don't you know that?" or try (and fail) to remember the name of some professor mentioned in some newspaper; and the keen rationalism of the modern mind will accept every word you say.

—G. K. Chesterton

In an ideal world, a non-Catholic's first impressions of the Catholic Church would be much more positive than they often are. In that happy world of mathematical perfection, an Evangelical could ask any passing Catholic a question about Catholic teaching and get a reasonable, informed answer. Conversation between Catholics and Evangelicals would be conducted at the level of pure theology and complete communication, instantly banishing many misunderstandings:

EVANGELICAL: [*Stirs sugar into teacup.*] Tell me, Friend Catholic, what your understanding is of the place of Mary in the economy of salvation? It would appear—though I could be wrong—that you worship her in some way. How do you reconcile this with the biblical witness that God alone is to be worshipped? [*Offers teacup to Catholic. Begins pouring his own cup and nodding in profound attentiveness throughout the following speech.*]

CATHOLIC: [*Takes teacup. Sips thoughtfully.*] Actually, Friend Evangelical, Catholics do not worship Mary. Rather, they accord her the

25

highest honor owing a mere creature (hyperdulia) while according God latria, the worship owing to God alone. This is not strange, since we all know what it is to honor a creature (such as our mother on Mother's Day) without honoring that creature to the same degree as God. Honor is, after all, a species of love and we know from the lips of Jesus himself that, far from insulting God, it is an act of love to God when we love our neighbor. Therefore, honoring Mary with hyperdulia is, in fact, an act of love that magnifies God's glory.

EVANGELICAL: [*Sips tea thoughtfully, nodding.*] Ah! I see! Lucidly spoken! Now, with respect to transubstantiation, I have the following inquiry . . .

Unfortunately, no travel agency sells tickets to that happy world. Instead, we live in this one, where people often rely on their own first impressions in making assessments of one another. And first impressions are, as the man said, deceiving.

How Most Evangelicals Meet the "Catholic Mary"

The Evangelical who seeks to find out what Catholics believe about Mary rarely gets a clear exposition of Marian piety and doctrine at the local parish. Nobody stands at the pulpit and says, "Today we're going to discuss the Church's dogmatic teaching on Mary. This will be followed by a thorough question-and-answer period. Noted biblical scholar and Mariologist Fr. Xavier Whosit of the Gregorian University will be flown direct from Rome to our parish coffee hour as a consultant."

Nope. When it comes to Mary, the first thing an Evangelical looks for is the last thing you get from Catholics at the parish level: a straightforward, biblical exposition of doctrine. Instead, what typically happens is something like this:

You walk into a Catholic Church and there's a statue of Mary. She's wearing a big gaudy crown and is standing on the world with a serpent underfoot. Or she's receiving a big gaudy crown from

God in some painting or stained-glass window. Sometimes, she's pictured holding a sort of miniature adult Jesus who is way way smaller than she is—as if she's more important than he is. Often, there are candles burning in front of a statue, icon, or painting of Mary. Or somebody is kneeling in front of a statue of her and, for all you can tell, praying to and worshipping it—or her.

Looking down on the supplicant with her big blue eyes, Mary's delicate northern European features and snow-white skin look terribly fragile and, well, weak. She looks as though she's about to burst into tears of sympathy for a child's bruised knee. If she could hear prayers (and, you remind yourself, she can't), you wonder how she could stand the strain of listening to the litany of human need and failure that must parade past her each day.

You turn around. Here's a bunch of people in the front row praying the Rosary after Mass. The score at the bottom of the first decade is Hail Mary: 10, Lord's Prayer: 1. So you know who is more important than our Father who art in Heaven.

You visit your Italian brother-in-law for Thanksgiving. He's the garage mechanic who wears the Miraculous Medal he got when he was confirmed fifteen years ago "for good luck."

You vaguely remember conversations with a guy you knew in sophomore English class in high school. He said he was in CCD classes until the priest and nun who taught at his parish ran off to get married in the late 1970s. He was part of the Stoner crowd and used to pray the Hail Mary when he was loaded. You asked him once at a party what that was all about and he couldn't tell you because he wasn't sure what the words meant but they made him feel "centered" when he was high.

You go to a Catholic co-worker's condo. He attends a suburban parish decorated with modern-looking art. He has a statue of Mary incongruously situated over the Bose Wave Radio on his enormous home entertainment center. The statue makes Mary look like a sort of Mother Courage rendered in the style of Soviet Realism. She's indefinably pan-Afro-Indian-Latino-Asian, rather than the Nordic Mary statue you saw at the church you visited, and she somehow looks ticked off and proud. Instead of whispering "There, there," she looks like she's about to seize a bullhorn and shout, "We're fierce! We're feminist! And we're in your face! That's Ms. Blessed Virgin Mary to you, buster!" She looks like she might go to a lot of foreign films about American aggression in the Third World when she's not running an organic food co-op and leading seminars on "Empowering Sisterhood."

The good news is that this guy doesn't strike you as somebody who worships Mary. The bad news is that he doesn't strike you as somebody who worships Jesus either (although he does say he finds certain kinds of meditation to be "spiritual"). He goes to Mass regularly, but says he's "got a lot of problems with the Church, like any big family." However, his problems with the Catholic faith are not quite the same as your problems with it. He's not just uncomfortable with the notion that the pope is infallible, he's uncomfortable with the notion that the Bible is inspired. He has problems with the Church's teaching on homosexual marriage, divorce, women priests, and all that "theological stuff," most of which he deems both boring and wrong. Like you, he thinks a lot of Catholic teaching is simply extra junk that has stuck to the main core of what Jesus came to say. But unlike you, he appears to think Jesus came to say "Be tolerant, support public television, and recycle," not "I came to die and rise for the sins of the world." Mostly your friend seems to think mainly in terms of politics, to see his Catholic faith as a sort of vehicle for social activism, and to regard the Mary statue as his symbol of solidarity with the oppressed. On the few occasions you've tried to probe him for information about Marian stuff, he gave you a blank look and said, "I don't know much about stuff like that. I was raised Catholic, but I don't think the Church should bog you down with all that philosophy. I think Catholics used to worship Mary, but I remember reading that all that went out with Vatican II. I think the doctrine of the Trinity also went out then, too. I dunno. Personally, I always thought the whole Virgin Birth thing was pretty silly. I mean, who knows what

happened? I'm not a Fundamentalist. I don't take the Bible literally."

So that doesn't set your mind at ease.

You go to the home of your Hispanic co-worker. This lady
is more devout and traditional. Her home looks a bit like a museum of Marian art. A painting of Mary holding baby Jesus is on
the wall. In the bathroom is another picture of Mary with her
heart exposed and a sword thrust through it. When you go to
get a beer out of the fridge, you notice an image of Our Lady of
Guadalupe precariously held to the door with magnets. A bunch
of Rosaries hang on a rack in the dining room with neat name tags
so the children can find their own Rosary for evening prayer. Your
friend has holy medals around her neck. She's got a big scrapbook
on her coffee table bulging with old pictures of May crownings,
christenings, and visits to Marian shrines like Lourdes and Fatima.
Her faith seems to be a mixture of elementary school catechesis
and affectionate folk piety that arouses some of your worst fears.
You try not to wince when she says, "Padre Pio used to tell that
story about how when Jesus closed the door to Heaven, Mama
Mary would let sinners in through the back window." She tells
you about people whose Rosaries supposedly turned to gold at
Medjugorje (whatever that is). If your friend is not Hispanic but
some other ethnicity, you might run into anything from an icon of
the Black Madonna to an image Our Lady of Knock to a Filipino
statue decked out in jewels and flowers.

That's what you start with as an Evangelical encountering the
Catholic relationship with Mary for the first time. And usually it
comes without a word of explanation from Catholics as to what all
these holy cards, icons, devotions, paintings, statues, rosaries and
whatnot mean. Worse still, you may soon realize to your horror
that many Catholics can't articulate what it's all about. That makes
you a sitting duck for anything that sounds plausible and seems
to fill in the blanks created by these inarticulate first impressions.
It makes you a sitting duck for pseudo-knowledge.

What's Pseudo-Knowledge?

Pseudo-knowledge is the stuff that "everybody knows," not because it's true, but because somebody with Important Hair said it on TV, or because your favorite magazine said so, or because a beloved character in a movie stated it as fact and lots of other people repeated it around millions of water coolers. Pseudo-knowledge is why "everybody knows" Humphrey Bogart said, "Play it again, Sam" (except he didn't). It's why "everybody knows" the Constitution speaks of a "wall of separation" between Church and State (except it doesn't). And it's why "everybody knows" medieval Europeans all believed the world was flat (except they didn't).[1] Pseudo-knowledge causes people to go around talking as though they must have read *The Federalist Papers*, or boned up on the meteorological data for global warming from the latest scientific studies, or committed to memory the documents of the Council of Trent, when they cannot, in fact, quote five words from any of these things. What they really know is what that resonant, well-modulated voice on TV or their own circle of friends (or both) told them was "common knowledge" concerning government or science or the Catholic Church.

Pseudo-knowledge may be harmless when its subject is no more important than the script of *Casablanca*. But pseudo-knowledge often becomes destructive when it comes to discussions of the Christian faith. A classic case in point is Dan Brown's novel, *The Da Vinci Code*. To any moderately informed reader, Brown's novel is ridiculous for many reasons, but I will focus on just one point briefly. Brown declares (and has repeated in interviews[2] that he is asserting this as fact, not as fictional license) that:

---

[1] Which is why Dante, the greatest poet of the Middle Ages, depicts himself passing through the center of earth and then emerging on Mount Purgatory on the other side of the globe in his *Divine Comedy*.

[2] Dan Brown, interview by Linda Wertheimer, *Weekend Edition*, NPR, April 26, 2003.

At [the Council of Nicea in A.D. 325] many aspects of Christianity were debated and voted upon—the date of Easter, the role of the bishops, the administration of sacraments, and, of course, the divinity of Jesus . . . until that moment in history, Jesus was viewed by his followers as a mortal prophet. . . . Jesus' establishment as the "Son of God" was officially proposed and voted on by the Council of Nicea. . . . A relatively close vote at that.[3]

LINDA WERTHEIMER: "How long does it take you to research a book like this? I assume that, among other things, you would hear from the world if you've got anything wrong."

DAN BROWN: "Certainly. And it takes me about two-and-a-half years to entirely research and write a book like this. Before I even started writing a page, I'd spent a year in research, and a lot of the research for *Angels and Demons* that I did in Vatican City played into this book, as well as my art history training in Seville."

LINDA WERTHEIMER: "You're trying not to get too fictional with the facts here?"

DAN BROWN: "Absolutely. The only thing fictional in *The Da Vinci Code* is the characters and the action that takes place. All of the locations, the paintings, the ancient history, the secret documents, the rituals, all of this is factual."

Dan Brown, interview by Martin Savidge, *CNN Sunday Morning*, CNN, May 25, 2003.

MARTIN SAVIDGE: ". . . When we talk about da Vinci and your book, how much is true and how much is fabricated in your storyline?"

DAN BROWN: "Ninety-nine percent of it is true. All of the architecture, the art, the secret rituals, the history, all of that is true, the Gnostic gospels. All of that is. All that is fiction, of course, is that there's a Harvard symbologist named Robert Langdon, and all of his action is fictionalized. But the background is all true."

Dan Brown, interview by Charles Gibson, *Good Morning America*, ABC News Transcripts, November 3, 2003.

CHARLES GIBSON: ". . . This is a novel. If you were writing it as a non-fiction book . . . how would it have been different?"

DAN BROWN: "I don't think it would have. I began the research for *The Da Vinci Code* as a skeptic. I entirely expected, as I researched the book, to disprove this theory. And after numerous trips to Europe, about two years of research, I really became a believer. And it's important to remember that this is a novel about a theory that has been out there for a long time."

[3] Dan Brown, *The Da Vinci Code* (New York: Doubleday, 2003), 233.

Brown's basic message: Jesus was just a dead rabbi who was all agog for the Sacred Feminine. His girlfriend, Mary Magdalene, was the true Holy Grail, since she bore the blood of Christ in the form of his descendants. All this was hushed up by the Evil Catholic Conspiracy, which took its marching orders from the pagan emperor Constantine. To consolidate Constantine's power, the Church allegedly ransacked paganism for all its ideas and suddenly declared Jesus to be God in order to control the stupid herd and stamp out the Sacred Feminine that had hitherto been the balancing force to the Sacred Masculine in paganism.

The hilarious thing about this claim is that it is self-refuting. After all, if everybody viewed Jesus as a mortal prophet until A.D. 325, then how can there be documents dating from nearly three centuries before Constantine which hail Jesus as the Son of God? Those documents are called the New Testament and, whether you believe them or not, they do date from the first century and they do say that Jesus Christ is "Lord and God." So somebody believed Jesus was the Son of God before Constantine. And others believed it enough to copy and circulate those original documents (not to mention read them to ever-swelling numbers of new Christians for three centuries before the Council of Nicaea).

Indeed, a paper trail a trained chimp could Google on the Internet shows that Christians constantly described Jesus as the Son of God in the three centuries before Constantine. In fact, even opponents of the faith writing decades before Constantine's birth knew this and made fun of it. Again, whether you believe Jesus is God is beside the point. What matters is that Brown is demonstrably wrong when he claims that Constantine grabbed a bunch of pagan mystery religion talking points, glued them on to the memory of a dead rabbi with a girlfriend, and magically transformed him into God.

Brown, at some level, appears to realize how dubious his claims are. To cover it all up, he performs a clever little shell game.

On the one hand, he tells us Constantine was the mastermind

who waged "a campaign of propaganda that demonized the Sacred Feminine, obliterating the goddess from modern religion forever."[4] Here Christianity is considered evil because it allegedly wiped out pre-Christian paganism that was uniformly worshipping goddesses as well as gods, since the ancients "envisioned their world in two halves—masculine and feminine."[5]

But at the same time, Brown states that Christianity is also the product of the pagan Constantine, who converted "sun-worshiping pagans to Christianity" by mingling paganism and the Jesus sect into a "hybrid religion."[6] In this case, Christianity is repackaged paganism and not actually about Christ.

Yet, in a final burst of incoherence, Brown claims that Christianity is also intolerant of paganism and launched a "smear campaign" against pagan goddesses, "recasting their divine symbols as evil. . . . In the battle between the pagan symbols and the Christian symbols, the pagans lost."[7] So we're back to the idea of Christianity being evil because it's actually not pagan but intolerantly Christian.

Doubly hilarious is that Brown's "proof" of this head-spinning nonsense is still more regurgitated pseudo-knowledge. He essentially steals the thesis of *Holy Blood, Holy Grail*, a work of pseudo-history that was laughed off the shelves by serious historians in the early 1980s. In addition, Brown asserts that the child Krishna was presented with gold, frankincense, and myrrh, and that Mithras was buried "in a rock tomb, and then resurrected in three days."[8] How does Brown know these things? Concerning Mithras' alleged death and resurrection, as well as the Christian "theft" of this idea, Carl Olson and Sandra Miesel write:

---

[4] *Ibid.*, 124.

[5] *Ibid.*, 36.

[6] *Ibid.*, 232.

[7] *Ibid.*, 37.

[8] Carl E. Olson and Sandra Miesel, *The Da Vinci Hoax* (San Francisco: Ignatius Press, 2003), 232.

That assertion apparently is taken (either directly or from a second-generation source) from Kersey Graves' *The World's Sixteen Crucified Saviors*,[9] a work of pseudo-scholarship and anti-Christian polemics that is so shoddy that many atheists and agnostics disavow it. Graves writes that several pagan deities, including " 'Mithra the Mediator' of Persia did, according to their respective histories, rise from the dead after three days' burial."[10] However, Graves provides no documentation as was his common practice (or non-practice).[11]

Likewise, when it comes to the claims about the Krishna/Christ nativity parallels, Olson and Miesel point out:

Graves conveniently provides no sources or citations, which is one of the many reasons his book has been long discredited by scholars working in the field of comparative religion. But that does not keep this popular idea from appearing on numerous web sites and in many popular esoteric books, with few (if any) providing sources or citations.[12]

Note that last sentence. Once again, Brown is relaying completely unsubstantiated pseudo-knowledge.

The trouble is, most readers of pulp fiction and most moviegoers are no more well-read about the history of Christianity than they are about *The Federalist Papers*. So they absorb Brown's claims, get snowed by the fake erudition of the novel, read the clippings from the *New York Daily News* anointing Brown an "impeccable" researcher,[13] read the copycat novels by hacks even more derivative than Brown, and watch a couple of TV shows featuring people

---

[9] Kersey Graves, *The World's Sixteen Crucified Saviors* (1875). Available at http://www.infidels.org/library/historical/kersey_graves/16/ as of August 15, 2007.

[10] *Ibid.*, chap. 19.

[11] Olson/Miesel, *The Da Vinci Hoax*, 151.

[12] *Ibid.*, 152.

[13] Bruno Blumenfeld, "Mystery," *New York Daily News*, December 22, 2001. Cited on the official web site of best-selling author Dan Brown (http://www.danbrown.com).

with well-modulated voices and Important Hair who treat this stuff seriously.

Result: Through the magic of pseudo-knowledge, polls have shown that large percentages of people (for instance, roughly 60% of British *Da Vinci* readers and viewers[14]) believe Brown's claims are reliable and repeat those claims as such. After just a few mornings around the water cooler, "everybody knows" Jesus was a dead rabbi with a girlfriend and some New Age ideas about the Sacred Feminine. Likewise, "everybody knows" Constantine is the bad guy who corrupted the true message of Jesus, and the Church is merely a collection of warmed-over pagan ideas.

Why Do People Buy This So Easily?

They buy it because Brown is confirming a fear and ratifying a prejudice. We live in a celebrity-obsessed culture fascinated with the sex lives (real and imagined) of the famous. We also live in an age which has seen the rise of feminism and which prizes something it calls "spirituality"—a Vast Tapioca Benevolence that affirms us in our okayness. But although people love spirituality in general, they often loathe the thought of a transcendent Father God who might bother us with commands and theology and "Thou shalt nots" and that irritating word, sin. And finally, we live in the post-Watergate age of the *X-Files*, in which Vast Conspiracies by Sinister Organizations are widely credited with little critical thought.

By some unfathomable coincidence, that's exactly what Dan Brown has packaged and sold: a guru with an active sex life who is all about Sacred Feminine paganism with its duality of god and goddess (and who is, of course, hushed up by the Evil Conspirato-

---

[14] According to a poll commissioned by the Da Vinci Code Response Group and available on the web site of the Roman Catholic Diocese of Westminster (http://www.rcdow.org.uk/davincicode/).

rial Church whose God is spoken of using the pronoun formerly known as "He").

In short, Brown simultaneously fans fears ("All the darkest things you've ever suspected about Christianity are true!") and flatters pride ("I will initiate you into the Secret History of our Time! I will save you from being one of the herd of suckers."). That's a heady brew, and it has made thirty million readers and millions more moviegoers who know little about actual Christianity drunk on pseudo-knowledge.

The trouble, I discovered, is that what's good enough for *Da Vinci Code* fans when it comes to our Lord is also good enough for most Evangelicals when it comes to our Lady.

Worlds in Collision

Imagine yourself channel surfing one evening. You flip over to EWTN, the all-Catholic-all-the-time TV network founded by Mother Angelica. Suppose you see the following ad, narrated by a man with a booming voice and a southern twang:

"Support Petros Ministries! Marching out in the power of the Spirit to claim victory over the powers of Hell! Anointed! Dynamic! Making an impact on this generation in the all-powerful, all-conquering Name of King Jesus!"

Doesn't sound very Catholic, does it?

Yet is there anything in the *Catechism of the Catholic Church*'s description of the mission of Catholics that's fundamentally at variance with the language above? No. Not a thing. Catholics are called to be soldiers for Christ. Just ask St. Ignatius Loyola, founder of the Jesuits. Catholics have it on the highest authority that the gates of Hell shall not prevail against the Church (cf. Matt. 16:18). Every Catholic is anointed with the Holy Spirit through faith in Christ Jesus (normally through Baptism and Confirmation). Catholics are indeed called to make a dynamic impact on our generation for Jesus. And yet Catholics just don't talk this way.

So, dazed from this strange experience with Catholic television, you keep channel surfing and find yourself wandering over to some sort of *Bible Gospel Hour.* The show cuts to a commercial and you hear an elegant English woman's voice say:

> "Read *The Inner Way of Silence* and allow God to invite you to enter more deeply into the path of contemplation. Experience sanctity as a fruit of dialogue with the Holy Spirit. Practice the presence of God and open yourself to the gentle promptings of the Spirit by saying, with the Bible, 'I am the handmaid of the Lord; let it be done unto me according to your word.' Allow the Spirit to breathe into your quiet reflection on the work of God in Scripture and creation. Let God bring forth in you, as in Mary's womb, the Christ who comes to us in prayer and mystery."

Again, you feel like you're in an alternate dimension, because no Evangelical talks this way. But is there anything in the theology of this ad that's unbiblical or opposed to Evangelical belief?

Again, not a thing. Sanctity is a fruit of the Holy Spirit. We are indeed called by Scripture to respond to God by saying, "Let it be to me according to your word." The Spirit does indeed breathe upon us and we are indeed to reflect on the work of God in Scripture and creation. The Bible even likens our formation in Christ to the formation of a child in its mother's womb (cf. Gal. 4:19). And of course, God does come to us in prayer and mystery.

So your strange trip to televisionland has left you with a pretty puzzle. You've watched Catholics say true things about their faith in ways almost no Catholic would say them. Likewise, you've seen Evangelicals say biblically true things in ways no Evangelical would say them. Even more puzzling is that both the Catholics and the Evangelicals are saying things that both would affirm to be true. What's wrong with this picture?

Masculine and Feminine, Evangelical and Catholic

Note the vocabulary in the first ad: anointed, dynamic, impact, marching, victory, all-conquering, king. Other favorite words in the Evangelical lexicon are mighty, battle, conquer, lordship, and so forth. Book blurbs, radio ads, and TV shows in the Evangelical world emphasize these words—words we usually gender-code as masculine.

In the second ad, the stress is on words like contemplation, inner life, receptivity, and openness. Catholic readers will recognize these and other buzzwords like invite, nurture, faith journey, dialogue, faith community, and share as common features of Catholic jargon. These are words we usually gender-code as feminine.

The gender-coding is what caused the disconnect between what we heard in the ads and what we know from experience. The first blurb dressed Catholic content in masculine language, while the second clothed Evangelical content in feminine language. That's why, once we peeled off the cultural trappings, we could find nothing in the Catholic ad that could not be affirmed by both Catholics and Evangelicals, just as there was nothing in the Evangelical ad that both could not affirm as well. Both ads are biblical, and both have roots in sacred Tradition. But since we are used to hearing Catholic culture—culture, mind you, not theology—expressed in feminine terms, and Evangelical culture—culture, mind you, not theology—expressed in masculine terms, it throws us for a loop.

So what's the point of this little thought experiment? Simply this: Before we ever get around to discussing substantial theological disagreements, Catholics and Evangelicals often mistake cultural differences for theological quarrels. Moreover, secular culture (which is hostile to both Catholic and Evangelical Christianity) often compounds the problem by feeding us its own stereotypes about both cultures. To be sure, this is not an All-Explaining Theory of Everything about Catholic/Evangelical disagreements.

There are, in addition to this phenomenon, plenty of real theological differences. But still, because this cultural difference is typically not noticed by either party, it sits there quietly operating and producing numerous misunderstandings and feelings of alienation on both sides before the theological discussion ever begins.

Such collisions can easily be spotted whenever one group unfairly caricatures the other. Take, for instance, different approaches to prayer. The feminine culture of the Catholic can predispose him to view the Evangelical approach to prayer as shallow and utilitarian. Buying into what "everybody knows" about Evangelicals based on media portrayals of Evangelicals as greedy, power-hungry hypocrites, some Catholics will assume Evangelical prayer uses God as a tool to achieve worldly ends ("Oh Lord, won't you buy me a Mercedes-Benz!").

Meanwhile, Evangelicals—buying into what "everybody knows" about Catholics based on media portrayals of sweet-faced, pious sitcom nuns and dim, nervous priests incapable of dealing with the real world—tend to see Catholic piety as an inarticulate inwardness cut off from real life. Thus, Evangelicals frequently criticize the Catholic faith for its "retreat from reality behind the walls of the cloister," where out-of-touch monks and nuns pray piously while ignoring their duties to claim the world for Jesus Christ.

The Catholic who is tempted to pass judgment needs to be reminded that petitionary prayer is commanded by our Lord ("Give us this day our daily bread" [Matt. 6:11]). The Evangelical who is tempted to pass judgment needs to be reminded that Jesus went into the desert to pray and seek union with the Father precisely for the purpose of saving the world, and that this is, in fact, what contemplative orders in the Catholic Church (like the Trappists) are all about. In short, both are legitimate forms of approach to God.

Similarly, Catholics should not dismiss Evangelicalism as simplistic chatter merely because Evangelicals tend to be more verbal about their faith. There is nothing noble or spiritual about the common lay Catholic's inability to be always ready to give an account of the hope within us (cf. 1 Pet. 3:15). Nor should Evangelicals think Catholics are "cold and dead" simply because they often don't manifest their deep relationship with Christ in a spontaneous, verbal, and outgoing way. The Evangelical needs to realize that not all "spontaneous" prayer is authentic contact with the living God, and that formal or liturgical prayer is not the same thing as a soulless ritual.[15]

Masculine, Feminine, and the Incarnation

Evangelicals, like all orthodox Christians, vigorously affirm the doctrine of the Incarnation—the faith of all Christians that God the Son, the Second Person of the Blessed Trinity, was conceived by the Holy Spirit in the womb of the Virgin Mary and became man. Evangelicals, like Catholics, believe this doctrine with every fiber of their being. But there's more to it than this. In Evangelical culture, "incarnation" tends to get prefaced with the singular word "the"—as in "The Incarnation." It's primarily seen as a single (albeit glorious) historical event, and its application to everyday Evangelical life usually has the character of a doctrine that is firmly believed. Catholics, while affirming the uniqueness of the Incarnation in the person of Jesus, also see Incarnation as an eternal reality to be lived and breathed by the followers of Jesus. They believe that God, in becoming human, was not simply performing an isolated miracle; he was establishing an eternal principle. In the Incarnation, Catholics believe, God was committing himself

---

[15] Back in my Evangelical days, I saw a cartoon in *The Wittenburg Door* featuring an earnest Evangelical hunched over in prayer with eyes clamped shut, pleading, "Oh Lord, I just really worship you and I just really want to come before you and just really pray that you would just really take the words just and really out of my prayer vocabulary." Not all spontaneous prayer is up to the glory of the task, and there is much wisdom in Catholics using the great and poetic prayers of the saints as their own.

to continually revealing his power and grace in and through human things. And the unfamiliar ways that Catholics express this belief tend to make Evangelicals very nervous.

This nervousness only gets compounded when popular Evangelicalism meets popular Catholicism. For the emphasis on seeing the Incarnation as a single event two thousand years ago on the other side of the earth often makes Evangelicals view it as an episode that ended with the Ascension of Christ into Heaven. Many Evangelicals speak as though the grace of God now reaches us only in "spiritual" (read: "disembodied") ways. Enfleshing that grace in people today is too much, too close.

This pattern of "that was then, this is now" can often be observed when Evangelicalism and Catholic faith meet. For example, it's not hard for Evangelicals to grant that God could unite himself with matter in the physical body of Jesus Christ, but the notion that he continues to do so through the consecrated bread and wine of the Eucharist is rejected as unbiblical and even magical or idolatrous—despite the fact that Jesus declared "This is my body, this is my blood" as Matthew, Mark, Luke, and Paul all record. Evangelicals find private confession of sins to God acceptable and even approve (generally) of accountability and discipleship. But the idea that a flesh-and-blood human being could have authority and power from Jesus to forgive sins in his name is typically declared unbiblical—even though Jesus conferred exactly this power on the apostles with the words, "If you forgive the sins of any, they are forgiven; if you retain the sins of any, they are retained" (John 20:23). Similarly, Evangelicals delight in the biblical picture of Jesus healing at the pool of Siloam by means of water (cf. John 9), but fret at the Catholic idea of holy water or blessed salts, since these seem somehow magical or fleshly. So do various other Catholic physical acts such as lighting candles to pray, or the gestures and prayers of the liturgy, which can strike some Evangelicals as mere rote.

Because Evangelicalism tends to see the Incarnation solely as an isolated historic event, not as the establishment of an eternal principle, the Evangelical tends to reply to the Catholic's confidence that God will use matter and people to communicate his grace by saying "God is spirit, and those who worship him must worship in spirit and truth" (John 4:24). The assumption is that spirit is spirit and matter is matter and never the twain shall meet (after the Ascension). There is a strong tendency to insist that all outward forms of what is generally termed "religion" are just distractions from spiritual worship. As Thomas Howard notes:

> Using Saint Paul's language about flesh and spirit, this piety has often spoken as though to be holy ("spiritual") is to be more or less disembodied. Since that is obviously not possible, we will do our best to keep spiritual things distinct from physical things. There will be "the spiritual life" and "the ordinary life." There will be sacred activities and secular activities. When we are praying, we are closer to the center of things than when we are washing dishes, changing diapers, driving in a traffic jam, or sitting in a committee meeting: thus would run this piety.
>
> This is to misread Saint Paul. He never meant his word spiritual to mean disembodied. To be spiritual for Saint Paul was to have brought everything back to God where it belongs and where it was in Eden. It is to have had one's life knit back together so that it is no longer secular and divided, but whole. It is to become one with Christ in whom dwells all the fullness of God bodily. Christ is the great icon and paradigm of this wholeness. In him we see the fullness of God in bodily form, and we are called to that wholeness, not to disembodied angelic life. The Christian religion, far from driving a wedge between them, knits the spiritual and the physical back together.[16]

And where does all this Incarnation—all this messiness of God taking on our creatureliness and revealing himself as a human person through human things in a very human way—begin? It begins with none other than the Blessed Virgin Mary who, after all, is the

---

[16] Thomas Howard, *Evangelical Is Not Enough* (Nashville, Tenn.: Thomas Nelson Publishers, 1984), 31–32.

source of Jesus' human nature. And curiously, it is Mary, the most Feminine of the Feminine—the *mater* out of whose substance God clothed himself in matter—who makes most Evangelicals steeped in the masculine way more nervous than almost anything else in the Catholic faith.

The Spectrum of Evangelical Reactions to Mary

Evangelical reactions to Mary form a kind of bell curve. On one end, you find the ferocious rhetoric of guys like Jack Chick, Dave Hunt, and various other fringe personalities who put the fun in Fundamentalism and who do not regard Catholics as Christian at all. Catholics should note that most Evangelicals also regard these guys as fringe extremists and don't share their vehement loathing of the Catholic Church. At the other end of the bell curve, you find Evangelicals who have a very high regard for the Catholic faith and who even long for the great Marian beauty they see in the Catholic communion, much as many Catholics long for the lay dynamism, apostolic zeal, and familiarity with Scripture they see in Evangelicalism. At this end of the bell curve, you find Evangelicals like Peter Toon writing:

> I felt this, for example, recently in the retreat center called Maison Riviere in Sherbrooke, Quebec. It is run by Roman Catholic Sisters, who are most caring and who have a deep devotion to the one they call "our Lady." I looked at books by a variety of authors on Mary, sat in the chapel, walked in the garden, and listened to the singing of the nuns, and as I did so, the question was deeply impressed on my mind: Am I missing something?[17]

That kind of reflection about Mary's place in the Christian life is unusual in Evangelicalism. And it leads to an even deeper thought, which Toon expresses poignantly:

---

[17] Peter Toon, "Appreciating Mary Today," in *Chosen by God: Mary in Evangelical Perspective*, ed. David F. Wright (London: Marshall Pickering, 1989), 224.

I must confess that I am deeply impressed by the way in which some of my favorite writers—Bernard, Francis de Sales, Anselm, and moderns like Hans Urs von Balthasar—have both a profound love for our Lord and a special love for Mary. Take for example this extract from a prayer of Anselm: "Surely Jesus, Son of God, and Mary His Mother, you both want, and it is only right, that whatever you love, we should love too. So, good Son, I ask you through the love you have for your Mother, that as she truly loves you and you her, you will grant that I may truly love her. Good Mother, I ask you by the love you have for your Son, that, as He truly loves you and you Him, you will grant that I may love Him truly."[18]

But for all his sympathy with the Catholic love of Mary, Toon can't help but add that, for reasons he himself doesn't fully understand, he feels he must hold back from her:

I ask myself: Why cannot I pray in this manner? Is there something lacking in my theological and spiritual appreciation that prevents me from regarding Mary in this way? And as yet I have found no satisfactory answers to my questions.[19]

And so Toon concludes his reflection wistfully:

Having offered what is, I hope, a warm, scriptural appreciation of Mary, I still cannot escape the feeling that there is more to say than I have said and more than we Evangelical Protestants normally say, even in our most generous moods and compassionate moments.[20]

Certainly in my experience (and, I think, in the experience of most Evangelicals), Toon has most emphatically said more than Evangelicals normally say about Mary and (if you ask the average Evangelical) a great deal too much besides.[21]

---

[18] Ibid.

[19] Ibid.

[20] Ibid.

[21] Though I am happy to report that Toon is not entirely alone, as is evidenced by Timothy George's excellent essay "The Blessed Evangelical Mary." Available at http://www.ctlibrary.com/ct/2003/december/1.34.html as of August 18, 2008.

For while the average Evangelical rejects the extremist notions of Chick, Hunt, and the whole fringe of anti-Catholic professionals who have nothing to say besides "The Catholic Church is evil!," he does think the Catholic view of Mary is at best highly problematic, and at worst a dangerous departure from biblical Christianity. Average Evangelicals—particularly since witnessing the pontificate of John Paul II, the life of Mother Teresa, and the valor of Catholics in the pro-life movement—embrace Catholics as fellow Christians and admire the fruits of the Spirit at work among Catholics. In fact, for many Evangelicals, there's often an element of "the grass is greener on the other side of the fence" desire for much that they see in Catholic life (as indeed there's much the same holy envy of Evangelicals among Catholics). But still, the average Evangelical strongly believes that Catholics labor under a number of false teachings—especially Marian teachings —that impede their relationship with Jesus Christ. Their attitude toward Catholics is somewhat like one's attitude toward a beloved but peculiar aunt who goes to church and believes in Jesus, but also watches those late-night TV shows with psychics and horoscopes and thinks there's something in reincarnation.

And so, for all the Church's attractions, Catholic devotion to Mary continues to give the overwhelming majority of Evangelicals what is commonly known as "the willies." Most Evangelicals are absolutely, positively certain the Catholic Church just honors Mary way too much and that there's something profoundly at odds with authentic Christianity in "the Catholic Mary." That's why an Evangelical authority like the *Christian Research Journal* could fret some years ago that "Mary is now 'back in style,'" and state that for this reason "the time has come for a Protestant response."[22] Note the emotional dynamic behind a statement like that. Its name in English is "fear."

After all, if someone told you happy families, walks in the

---

[22] Elliot Miller, "The Mary of Roman Catholicism," *Christian Research Journal* (Summer 1990), 9–15; (Fall 1990) 27–33.

woods, beautiful music, children, and loving one's mother "de-manded a response," you'd think he was very odd, since those are all good things. This kind of response reveals a habitual mental posture toward Mary: namely, that she's not a good thing. Instead, she is, first and foremost, a danger. Otherwise, the mainstream Evangelicalism so typically represented by the *Christian Research Journal* would welcome Mary being back in style, not feel a need to respond, just as mainstream Evangelicalism welcomed Jesus being brought back in style with the debut of *The Passion of the Christ* and didn't feel any demand for a "Protestant response."

Why is the "Catholic Mary" regarded as a danger? Because she is assumed to be, in a word, pagan. And thereby hangs another tale of pseudo-knowledge.

Why Evangelicals Assume Catholic Marian Teaching Must Be Pagan

As an Evangelical, I shared this visceral fear of Mary. Marian doc-trine and devotion seemed to be a mountain of invention built on a molehill of Scripture. After all, apart from the Magnificat (cf. Luke 1:46–55), a couple of incidents in the Gospel of John and the book of Acts, and the infancy narratives found in the Gospels of Matthew and Luke, Mary didn't seem nearly as important to the authors of the New Testament as she was to Catholics. And given the rather alien feminine atmosphere of Catholicism, it was easy and natural to conclude that, since the biblical information about Mary is apparently so meager, the only explanation for Catholic Marian piety and doctrine was that the Catholic Church must have imported it from somewhere else. And that somewhere else could only be paganism.

For the same reason, Dr. Norman Geisler writes that "in going beyond Scripture in her teachings about Mary, Roman Catholics have threatened Scripture as the sole authority for the faith"[23] and concludes with total confidence that the dogma of the Assumption is therefore "little more than baptized paganism." Likewise, Kenneth Samples and Elliot Miller, in a relatively good-natured attempt to discuss Mary from an Evangelical perspective, take it as axiomatic that Catholic teaching about Mary springs from "pagan soil."[24]

Geisler, Samples, and Miller aren't alone in this view. Indeed, it's profoundly normal in Evangelicalism to assume that Catholic ideas about Mary are derived mostly from paganism. Certainly I and the vast majority of my Evangelical friends took it as a settled fact that after the apostles died, unconverted or partially-converted pseudo-Christians began to import the goddess worship of their native cultures into a church that had stopped reading the Bible. The whole Mary thing seemed a classic example of what I termed "Pagan Creep"—whereby the pure New Testament Church was infiltrated by unbiblical ideas that seeped in from surrounding pagan culture. We were not clear on the exact chronology or process of this corruption, but there was no doubt it had happened on a broad scale. We could see nothing in Scripture saying, "Mary was an immaculate and sinless virgin all her life, until she was assumed bodily into Heaven. So let's all pray to the Mother of God!" And since none of that is spelled out in Scripture, it couldn't be Christian; therefore it must—simply must—be pagan. All the best authorities said so. And they were backed up by well-modulated voices on TV and radio. You could find the same thing verified in a thousand Evangelical magazines, book, and sermons. Everybody knew it was common knowledge.

---

[23] Elliot Miller and Kenneth Samples, *The Cult of the Virgin: Catholic Mariology and Apparitions* (Grand Rapids, Mich.: Baker Book House, 1992), foreword by Norman Geisler, 11.

[24] *Ibid.*, 67.

2

The Myth of the Pagan Mary

There is no there there.

—Gertrude Stein

At the scholarly level, Evangelical language reflecting this deep conviction of the pagan origins of Marian teaching and devotion tends to be gentle and muted, as it is with Geisler, Miller, and Samples. At the popular level, however, it tends to be much more harsh and blunt, even among generally respected preachers such as John MacArthur:

> The Roman Catholic view of Mary is pagan, it is utterly pagan. . . . It is bizarre, it is wrong, it is unbiblical to turn this humble servant of God (Mary) into the "queen of Heaven"—which Rome has done (the Roman Catholic Church). It is unthinkable to do such an idolatrous act. There is no queen in Heaven, there is only a King —there is no queen in Heaven, only the One, True, Eternal King! To say that Heaven has a queen, is to create an idol. Worship of Mary is idolatry—nothing less. Mary is not the queen of Heaven; Heaven has no queen. Heaven is occupied by a King who is a Trinity—Heaven is not a holy quartet—it is a Trinity.
>
> Now, the Roman Catholic Church didn't invent the idea of the queen of Heaven, they borrowed it from paganism. Turn to Jeremiah 7—it has nothing to do with Christianity, it never has, it is a pagan concept—it goes way back into Old Testament history.[1]

---

[1] John MacArthur, Jr., "The Virgin Birth: A Divine Miracle?" (lecture, Grace Community Church, Panorama City, Calif.), transcribed by Tony Capoccia and available at http://biblebb.com/files/mac/marycult.htm as of September 29, 2008.

Or among not-so-respected, but still enormously popular preachers like Jimmy Swaggart:

> The image of mother and child had been a primary object of Babylonian worship for centuries before the birth of Christ. From Babylon, this spread to the ends of the earth. The original mother figure in this tableau was Semiramis—the personification of unbridled lust and sexual gratification. And once we start to study the worship practices of heathen nations, we find amazing similarities embraced over wide areas and through long periods of time.
>
> These nations all trace their common worship from Babylon—before its dispersion in the days of Nimrod. *Thus, worship of Mary is Babylonian in origin. There is absolutely no suggestion of such worship in Scripture.*[2]

Now you may wonder how it is that Jimmy Swaggart—who is not known for his studies of the culture, history, and religion of ancient Babylon, nor for his command of cuneiform writing—knows so much about the roles of Semiramis and Nimrod in Babylonian religious practice. As it turns out, Swaggart didn't exactly discover all this on his own. Instead, he's repeating—without attribution—a claim made by Loraine Boettner in his great One-Stop-Shopping-Book-for-All-Your-Reasons-the-Catholic-Church-Is-Pagan entitled *Roman Catholicism.*[3] In other words, Swaggart is reciting something "everybody knows." And it was seeing that employment of pseudo-knowledge at work in my own Evangelical background that gave me the kick-start I needed to rethink my ideas about Mary.

---

[2] Jimmy Swaggart, *Catholicism and Christianity* (Baton Rouge: Jimmy Swaggart Ministries, 1986), 103–4; emphasis in original.

[3] Loraine Boettner, *Roman Catholicism* (Philadelphia: Presbyterian & Reformed Publishing Co., 1974), 136.

Pseudo-Knowledge in Popular Evangelical Critiques of Catholic Teaching

For I had already discovered that Boettner is a great fount of worthless claims and pseudo-knowledge about the supposed pagan origins of the Catholic faith. For instance, he offers a list of alleged "Roman Catholic inventions" that overwhelms us with charges which compensate for their lack of importance and basic honesty by the sheer force of numbers. Over and over we run into outright errors of fact such as:

- Latin used in worship—A.D. 600 (*So why did Jerome translate the Bible into Latin two hundred years before A.D. 600? And what does this claim signify, anyway? If most people spoke Latin at that time, why shouldn't Latin have been used in worship? Does Boettner find it sinister that English is used in worship today?*)

- Prayers for the dead—A.D. 300 (*This will certainly come as news to Judas Maccabeus who prayed for the dead over four centuries earlier. See 2 Macc. 12:42–45.*)

- Council of Valencia places the Bible on the Index of Forbidden Books—A.D. 1229 (*There was no Council of Valencia in 1229, In fact, Valencia was in Moorish hands at the time.*)

Or items of numbing inconsequence like:

- Wax candles—A.D. 320 (*Response: Why does this matter? How does Boettner know wax candles were first used in A.D. 320? Given that the use of electricity was still far in the future and that worship frequently occurred before sunrise so Christian slaves could attend, how else does Boettner expect the Christians to have read Scripture in the dark?*)

- College of Cardinals begun—A.D. 927 (*Response: Actually, the term "College of Cardinals" dates from the mid-twelfth century.*

> *Cardinals elect the pope. The office was created to protect papal elections from outright meddling by rival Italian clans. It was a creation of human ingenuity in response to a particular need, much like an Evangelical church's finance council, or a Board of Elders being charged with finding the new pastor at the Baptist church down the street. So why is this particular bit of administrative innovation significant?*)

- Baptism of bells instituted by Pope John XIII—A.D. 965 (*Response: "Baptism of bells" refers to a common custom of christening church bells. It's about as dastardly as breaking a bottle of champagne against the bow of a ship.*)

Now the interesting thing is that The List has been a staple on the Internet for so many years that the vast majority of the people who regurgitate it don't even know where it originates. Yet it continues to circulate, like a bad penny—or like Kersey Graves' *The World's Sixteen Crucified Saviors* circulates among Dan Brown disciples. A quick Google search reveals hundreds of sites reprinting The List and I've been sent countless e-mail regurgitations of it. The e-mails are usually accompanied by unconsciously ironic admonitions to "think for yourself and stop letting others tell you what to believe" from people who are completely unaware they're parroting something they've never thought about or checked out for themselves. Such people typically seem to assume "If there are so many claims against the Catholic Church, it stands to reason there must be something to the idea that Catholic doctrines are basically pagan." But the reality is that o x o x o x o = o, not "If you throw enough mud, some will stick." The reality also includes, "You shall not bear false witness against your neighbor," as Christians ought to know.

Catholics are not without a sense of humor about all this, of course. A friend of mine[4] once concocted a playful "Protestant

---

[4] Michael Lounsbery, in private correspondence with the author.

Inventions List" in response to his receiving the umpteenth e-mail of The List. It runs, in part:

A.D. 90:   Sunday worship taught by Didache
A.D. 180:   God first declared as a "Trinity" of three persons by Theophilus
A.D. 381:   Prayer to the Holy Spirit authorized by Council of Constantinople
A.D. 397:   Book of Revelation (until now dubious) proclaimed to be "Scripture"
A.D. 400:   Augustine invents "original sin"
A.D. 418:   Salvation apart from Jesus declared heretical by Pope Zosimus
A.D. 431:   Ephesus declares Mary's human son to be God himself
A.D. 525:   Calendar for Easter Sunday instituted
A.D. 950:   Invention of Bible in English
A.D. 1215:   Declaration that God created the world "out of nothing"
A.D. 1455:   Scheme for printing the Bible invented by Gutenberg
A.D. 1760:   Singing of "Amazing Grace" instituted by John Newton
A.D. 1776:   Protestant Founders of America downgrade Blessed Trinity to "Nature's God"
A.D. 1825:   Altar calls instituted by Charles Finney
A.D. 1863:   U.S. government enforces Thanksgiving to God as official state holiday
A.D. 1864:   Mammon worship first authorized by United States government. "In God We Trust" stamped on U.S. money
A.D. 1900:   Light bulbs used in worship services
A.D. 1929:   Wednesday night Bible study invented
A.D. 1951:   Preachers begin to dress in polyester suits
A.D. 1959:   Televangelism instituted by Pat Robertson
A.D. 1965:   "Four Spiritual Laws" promulgated by Bill Bright
A.D. 1969:   Unbiblical phrase "Accept Jesus Christ into your heart as your personal Lord and Savior" popularized
A.D. 1970:   Overhead projectors used in worship service
A.D. 1978:   Abortion declared to be a grave sin by Evangelicals and Fundamentalists

A.D. 1991: "Promise Keepers" founded on pattern of neo-pagan
          "men's groups"
A.D. 1998: Sale and commercialization of WWJD bracelets
A.D. 2001: "Faith-based" government founded by George W. Bush

His list is, of course, a deliberately silly concoction of inconsequential items, legitimate developments of doctrine, sinister-sounding (but harmless) adaptations of the Christian life to different cultural circumstances, and laughable twisting of fact. However, it's also an instructive rejoinder that points out an important truth: We do need to think for ourselves—particularly about what "everybody knows" concerning the "pagan origins" of Catholic teaching. For this peculiar pattern of endlessly circulating and re-circulating absurd and sinister-sounding "facts" about the Catholic faith is very common in Evangelicalism when it comes to Catholic beliefs about Marian devotion and doctrine.

Take, for instance, this telltale little factoid: One Joseph Zacchello "rebuts" what Catholics allegedly believe about prayers to Mary by declaring confidently that

using the Catholic population at the time he wrote
(the mid-1940s)

+

estimating one Hail Mary takes at least ten seconds

+

assuming half the world's Catholics say
at least one Hail Mary per day

+

allowing a certain amount of time for Rosaries, litanies, etc.

=

a low estimate of Mary listening to "46,296 petitions every second of time from one end of the year to the other, or, in other words . . . 46,296 petitions at one and the same time, simultaneously."[5]

Oddly enough, this exact same statistic of 46,296 prayers to Mary per second shows up without attribution on page twenty-four of another book that has wielded considerable influence in Evangelical opinions about the Catholic understanding of Mary: Ralph Woodrow's *Babylon Mystery Religion*. What are the odds that Woodrow did his own calculations and arrived at that exact same figure independently? I'd say about 46,296 to 1 myself. Clearly, Woodrow's "research" consisted of regurgitating a number he'd picked up either from Zacchello or from some other source that repeated Zacchello—much like Dan Brown regurgitated the bogus "research" of *Holy Blood, Holy Grail* or Kersey Graves' unsubstantiated junk about Mithras, Krishna, and Christ.

Woodrow's reliance on pseudo-knowledge wasn't confined to Zacchello's invented statistics. He also read and uncritically repeated the claims of an even earlier book called *The Two Babylons*, published in 1853 by Alexander Hislop. Hislop's book is one of the chief sources of supposed evidence that Catholic teaching about Mary comes from paganism and, in particular, from Babylon.

An example of Hislop's/Woodrow's logic is this: At Ephesus in A.D. 431, an ecumenical council declared Mary *Theotokos*, Greek for "God-bearer" or "Mother of God." This is true. But then Woodrow explains the sinister reason why:

At Ephesus? It was in this city that Diana had been worshiped as the goddess of virginity and motherhood from primitive times! She was said to represent the generative powers of nature and so was

---

[5] Joseph Zacchello, *Secrets of Romanism* (Neptune, N.J.: Loizeaux Brothers, 1948), 130.

pictured with many breasts. A tower-shaped crown, a symbol of the tower of Babel, adorned her head.[6]

And so, Woodrow says, we must conclude:

> When beliefs are held by a people for centuries, they are not easily forsaken. So Church leaders at Ephesus—as the falling away [from true Christianity] came—also reasoned that if people would be allowed to hold their ideas about a mother goddess, if this could be mixed into Christianity and the name Mary substituted, they could gain more converts.[7]

Woodrow also warns us about Marian iconography:

> The Egyptian goddess of fertility, Isis, was represented as standing on the [crescent moon] with stars surrounding her head. In Roman Catholic churches all over Europe may be seen pictures of Mary exactly the same way! The accompanying illustration below (as seen in Catholic catechism booklets) pictures Mary with twelve stars circling her head and the crescent moon under her feet![8]

There are two things to notice here. The first, which Woodrow eventually realized himself, is that in his zeal to discover paganism at the root of Catholic Marian theology, he neglected to notice this imagery is not actually found in Egyptian art (because Isis is never represented as standing on the crescent moon with stars surrounding her head). Rather, the imagery is found in Sacred Scripture:

> And a great portent appeared in Heaven, a woman clothed with the sun, with the moon under her feet, and on her head a crown of twelve stars; she was with child and she cried out in her pangs of birth, in anguish for delivery (Rev. 12:1−2).

---

[6] Ralph Woodrow, *Babylon Mystery Religion* (Riverside, Calif.: Ralph Woodrow Evangelistic Association, Inc., 1981), 17.

[7] *Ibid.*

[8] *Ibid.*, 19.

This, and the discovery of a hundred other inconsistencies and invented "facts" is why Woodrow, to his great credit, came to disavow his own work and has now published *The Babylon Connection?*,[9] correcting his own false assertions and debunking Alexander Hislop's *The Two Babylons*.

But the second and far more important thing to notice is this: the assumption that Marian devotion is pagan still lives on through the same process of repeating what "everybody knows" that Woodrow used in writing *Babylon Mystery Religion*. A quick Google search shows that eight years after Woodrow himself repudiated his own book, *Babylon Mystery Religion* is still cited on hundreds of sites, still continues to be sold by Christian booksellers, and still continues to be regarded as authoritative research on how "the Roman Catholic church permits the worship of the pagan mother goddess under the name of Jesus' mother Mary."[10] It's another textbook example of the way pseudo-knowledge propagates.

Indeed, two years after Woodrow completely rejected and debunked his own work and Hislop's *The Two Babylons*, Tim LaHaye, author of the enormously popular *Left Behind* series, wrote that "the greatest book ever written on [Babylonian religion] is the masterpiece *The Two Babylons*. . . . This book, containing quotations from 275 authors and to my knowledge never refuted, best describes the origin of religion in Babylon and its present-day function."[11]

And how did all this paganization happen, according to LaHaye? Carl Olson[12] sums up LaHaye's charge:

---

[9] *Op cit.*, *The Babylon Connection?*

[10] To quote one web site chosen at random: http://bupc.montana.com/whores/marywors.html as of August 15, 2007.

[11] Tim LaHaye, *Revelation Unveiled* (Grand Rapids, Mich.: Zondervan, 1999), 266.

[12] Carl Olson, "LaHaying the Rapture on Thick," *Envoy Magazine*, vol. 5.3. Available at http://www.envoymagazine.com/backissues/5.3/rapture.htm as of September 25, 2008.

Claiming that the Roman emperor Constantine's "profession of
faith" was a sham, LaHaye and Jenkins detail the kinds of "corruption" that eventually entered the once-pure early Church: "prayers
for the dead, making the sign of the cross, worship of saints and
angels, instituting the mass, and worship of Mary—which in the
church of Rome was followed by prayers directed to Mary, leading
to the 1950 doctrine of her assumption into Heaven and in 1965
to the proclamation that Mary was 'the Mother of the Church.' "[13]

St. Augustine is glibly described as a "Greek humanist" whose
introduction of "man's wisdom" further "pav[ed] the way for
more pagan thought and practice." Furthermore, St. Augustine's
"spiritualizing of Scripture eventually removed the Bible as the
sole source of authority for correct doctrine. At the same time,
the Scriptures were locked up in monasteries and museums, leav-
ing Christians defenseless against the invasion of pagan and hu-
manistic thought and practices. Consequently, the Dark Ages
prevailed, and the Church of Rome became more pagan than
Christian."[14]

Sound Familiar?

Just as Dan Brown did, LaHaye trots out Constantine as the all-
purpose villain. As in *The Da Vinci Code*, LaHaye makes the vague
and confused charge that Constantine somehow paganized Christianity. In a curiously happy concord, LaHaye and Brown are in
perfect agreement about one thing: the Catholic Church is a giant
conspiracy against the Truth and it's all Constantine's fault. Only
one blank space remains to be filled, and that's where "the Truth"

[13] Tim LaHaye and Jerry B. Jenkins, *Are We Living in the End Times? Current
Events Foretold in Scripture . . . And What They Mean* (Wheaton, Ill.: Tyndale,
1999), 173–74.
[14] *Ibid.*, 174.

can be found. Are Constantine and the Catholic Church evil because they suppressed the worship of the Sacred Feminine and invented the worship of Jesus, as Dan Brown says? Or are they evil because they suppressed the worship of Jesus and invented the worship of the Sacred Feminine in the person of Mary, as LaHaye says? No matter, as long as we accept without question what "everybody knows"—that Constantine and sundry sinister agents corrupted "real" Christianity with the false teachings of the Catholic faith.

If this sounds disturbingly close to the "pagan creep" scenario, that's because it is the "pagan creep" scenario. And it raises the same question: If Brown's pseudo-knowledge argument is bogus when it comes to Jesus, why is the same argument sound when it comes to Evangelical views of Mary? How, precisely, had we Evangelicals come to think the "Catholic Mary" was pagan?

Because Hislop, Boettner, Woodrow, MacArthur, LaHaye, Samples, Geisler, Miller, the *Christian Research Journal* and, oh, everybody "just knows" that Catholic devotion to Mary is "little more than baptized paganism." Because it's "common knowledge." Because thousands of Web site authors repeat it to one another. Because Mary gives us the willies. Because all those holy cards, statues, candles, Rosaries, and so forth just seemed weird. Because you can hear "The Catholic Mary comes from pagan soil" in a thousand Evangelical sermons, read it in a thousand Evangelical books and magazines, and hear it on a thousand Evangelical TV and radio shows. Because we can't see the biblical basis for all of it, and so it must—simply must—be pagan. And even though Woodrow has repudiated his own work and exploded Hislop's theories, even though LaHaye depends on Hislop, even though Swaggart depends on the factually-challenged Boettner, and even though Samples, Miller, and Geisler don't offer a particle of hard evidence at all, it remains "common knowledge" among us Evangelicals that Marian devotion and doctrine are fundamentally pagan in origin because, well, it's common knowledge.

The Phantom Apostasy

I shared that opinion for years. But as I began to study what the Catholic Church actually teaches instead of what "everybody knows" the Church teaches, I began to discover something: the difficulty with the "pagan creep" theory is how to pin it down to specifics. When exactly did this paganization take place? Who were its perpetrators? What precisely are the sources from which pagan beliefs entered the Church? If Constantine (who lived in the fourth century) is the culprit who introduced "Mary worship" and other pagan innovations into the Church, as LaHaye claims, why does the Christian writer Irenaeus (writing circa A.D. 180) sound just like a Catholic when he says Mary is the "Second Eve" who, "being obedient, was made the cause of salvation for herself and for the whole human race"?[15] If the dogma of Mary as *Theotokos* or "God-Bearer" was imported from Diana-worship at the Council of Ephesus in A.D. 431, why is Irenaeus (who lives in Lyons in Gaul, over two thousand miles from Ephesus) writing 250 years earlier that "The Virgin Mary . . . being obedient to his word, received from an angel the glad tidings that she would bear God"?[16]

My problem, both in looking at the Church before I entered it and in looking at Mary afterwards, was that I'd encountered this sort of thing before and had discovered that trying to find the date for the paganization of True Christianity was like trying to grab a fistful of smoke. As an Evangelical committed to the "pagan creep" theory, reading Irenaeus' very Catholic-sounding words meant I had to backdate my theory again and look for the paganization of True Christianity sometime around A.D. 180.

But when I did, I discovered that other Catholic-sounding doctrines, such as belief in the Eucharist as the literal flesh and blood

---

[15] Irenaeus, *Adversus Haereses*, 3, 22, 4.

[16] *Ibid.*, 5, 19, 1.

of Christ, or belief in bishops as the successors to the apostles (both of which I had also been assured were pagan ideas), were found in the writings of Ignatius of Antioch[17] (c. A.D. 107) and Clement of Rome[18] (c. A.D. 80). If I was going to hold my "pagan creep" theory, I'd have to backdate it even further and posit that an almost-complete corruption of Christianity from east to west had occurred even before John put the period at the end of the last sentence in the book of Revelation: Because during the very lifetime of John the apostle, you've got Clement, the bishop of Rome, talking about apostolic succession just like a Catholic (and getting no quarrel from anybody). You've also got him acting like, well, the pope: writing to a far-off city (Corinth) and speaking as though he has the pastoral authority to tell them to behave themselves. But instead of burning the letter, the Corinthians treasure it and even circulate copies to other churches.

It's the same deal with Ignatius' writings. It's not just that Ignatius regards the Eucharist as the literal body and blood of Christ, like a Catholic would; rather, it's that everybody else agrees with him for the next thousand years! Ignatius' letters, instead of being burnt as heresy by the true disciples of the apostles, are saved and

---

[17] Ignatius tells his flock that one of the marks of false teachers is that "[f]rom Eucharist and prayer they hold aloof, because they do not confess that the Eucharist is the Flesh of our Savior Jesus Christ, which suffered for our sins, and which the Father in his loving-kindness raised from the dead" (Ignatius, *Letter to the Smyrnaeans*, 7, 1).

[18] "The apostles received the gospel for us from the Lord Jesus Christ; and Jesus Christ was sent from God. Christ, therefore, is from God, and the apostles are from Christ. Both of these orderly arrangements, then, are by God's will. Receiving their instructions and being full of confidence on account of the Resurrection of our Lord Jesus Christ, and confirmed in faith by the word of God, they went forth in the complete assurance of the Holy Spirit, preaching the good news that the kingdom of God is coming. Through countryside and city they preached; and they appointed their earliest converts, testing them by the Spirit, to be the bishops and deacons of future believers" (Clement, *Letter to the Corinthians*, 42, 1–4).

recopied so Christians all over the ancient world could read them. And rightly so, since Ignatius is the model Christian martyr. He prefers—as he wrote on his way to the Coliseum—to be "ground by the teeth of wild beasts, so that I may become the pure bread of Christ."[19] Ignatius' crime: he refused to compromise with paganism in any way.

Likewise, we've got the witness of another second century Christian, Polycarp of Smyrna. Polycarp actually knew the apostle John and belonged to a church that was most emphatically not drifting away from Jesus, if Jesus' own assessment counts for anything:

> And to the angel of the church in Smyrna write: "The words of the first and the last, who died and came to life.
>
> "I know your tribulation and your poverty (but you are rich) and the slander of those who say that they are Jews and are not, but are a synagogue of Satan. Do not fear what you are about to suffer. Behold, the devil is about to throw some of you into prison, that you may be tested, and for ten days you will have tribulation. Be faithful unto death, and I will give you the crown of life. He who has an ear, let him hear what the Spirit says to the churches. He who conquers shall not be hurt by the second death" (Rev. 2:8–11).

Polycarp obeys Jesus to the letter by choosing to be burnt at the stake rather than abandon our Lord. *The Martyrdom of Polycarp*, written by eyewitnesses shortly after the event, tells us:

> When the Proconsul urged him and said, "Take the oath and I will release you; revile Christ," Polycarp answered: "Eighty-six years I have served him, and he has never done me wrong. How, then, should I be able to blaspheme my King who has saved me?"

These are not the words of a man inclined to compromise with paganism or import a little goddess worship into the gospel to spice it up a bit for Diana-worshipers. On the contrary, they're

---

[19] Ignatius, *Letter to the Romans*, 4, 1.

the words of someone who, according to a man who knew him personally, was

> instructed not only by the apostles, and conversed with many who had seen Christ, but was also appointed bishop of the church in Smyrna, by the apostles in Asia. I saw him in my early youth; for he tarried a long time, and when quite old he departed this life in a glorious and most noble martyrdom. He always taught those things which he had learned from the apostles, and which the Church had handed down, and which are true. To these things all the churches in Asia bear witness, as do also the successors of Polycarp even to the present time.[20]

This writer had profound admiration for Polycarp's steadfast resistance to those who wanted to replace the word of God with mere human wisdom. One of these people was a guy named Marcion.

> Once he was met by Marcion who said to him, "Do you recognize me?" and Polycarp replied, "I recognize you as the firstborn of Satan!"[21]

Why was Polycarp so harsh with Marcion? Because Marcion claimed the Old Testament was the product of the evil god of the Jews. He preached that Jesus Christ was the good God (a pure spirit being who only appeared to be human). Marcion's big hero was Paul, but he taught that various sinister influences had corrupted Paul's writings (does this sound familiar?). Only instead of blaming Constantine (who wouldn't be born for more than a century), Marcion attributed the corruption to a Jewish conspiracy. Marcion obligingly deleted the Old Testament from Scripture and rewrote the New Testament until it said what he wanted it to say. All quotes from the Old Testament were deleted from Paul's writings and only ten Pauline letters were allowed into Marcion's Sanitized-For-Your-Protection Version of the Bible, along with a heavily-edited Gospel of Luke. Marcion created a Jesus who fit

---

[20] Irenaeus, *Adversus Haereses*, 3, 3, 4.

[21] *Ibid.*

his prejudices against Jews and his penchant for borrowing trendy ideas from Greco-Roman and Gnostic thought.

Now, if the early Church was, as I had thought, all agog for importing paganism as quickly as possible and ignoring the Bible, Marcion should have been made a saint. Instead, the early Church agreed that Marcion had "a pumpkin . . . in place of a brain"[22] and denounced him furiously.

In fact, one of the Church Fathers responded to Marcion's attack on Scripture in two ways: First, he promulgated the first canon or official list of Scripture in the history of the Church so that his confused flock in Lyons could know which writings were scriptural and thus be protected against Marcion's editing. That list not only re-affirms the Old Testament pretty much as we have it today, but largely resembles our present New Testament canon as well.

Second, this fellow wrote an extensive treatise called *Against Heresies* that catalogued and refuted the various ways his contemporaries attempted to ignore Scripture and importing pagan ideas into the faith. This, by the way, was the same man who recorded Polycarp's vehement words to Marcion previously noted. He was also the same man who struggled to bring a man named Florinus back to the faith by urging him to emulate the courage and faith of Polycarp, with the reminder that they had both known the great martyr and received the gospel from him, just as Polycarp had heard the gospel from the lips of John the apostle himself:

> I remember the events of those days better than the ones of recent years. What a boy learns grows with the mind and becomes a part of him, so that I am able to describe the very place in which the blessed Polycarp sat as he discoursed, his goings and his comings, the manner of his life, his physical appearance, as well as the discourses he delivered to the people, and how he spoke of his familiar conversation with John and with the rest of those who had seen the Lord, and how he would recall their words to mind. All that

---

[22] Tertullian, *Against Marcion*, 4, 40, 3.

he had heard from them concerning the Lord or about his miracles and about his teaching, having received it from eyewitnesses of the Word of Life, Polycarp related in harmony with the Scriptures.[23]

So who is this bulwark against heresy, this champion of Scripture, this tireless opponent of the corruption of Christianity?

His name is Irenaeus of Lyons—the same Irenaeus who lovingly speaks of Mary as the Second Eve, the Bearer of God, and "the cause of salvation for herself and for the whole human race."

The Early Church: Biblical, Orthodox, and Marian

As an Evangelical, this took me aback. For a long time, I could not account for the gigantic gap between my assumption that Marian devotion and doctrine was the product of pagans and the fact that Irenaeus held paganism in contempt. Nor could I account for the fact that Irenaeus was not alone. For what marks the early Church Fathers is not disrespect for Scripture, a fondness for paganism, or a wistful longing for the good old days of Isis and Athena. Rather, it is a general contempt for pagan deities, a profound immersion in Scripture, and an ever-deepening devotion to Mary.

For instance, St. Athanasius, the great fourth century lion of orthodoxy, writes a treatise called *Against the Pagans* while simultaneously avowing that Mary is "ever-virgin"[24]—two centuries before the dogma of Mary's Perpetual Virginity is proclaimed by the Church. Likewise, St. Augustine authors *The City of God Against the Pagans* for the express purpose of showing that the gods of paganism are false and the God of Christianity is real. He's the man who insists, louder than anybody else in the ancient world, on fidelity to the scriptural teaching that "all have sinned and fallen short of the glory of God" (Rom. 3:23), and on the absolute necessity of God's unmerited grace in Jesus Christ for

---

[23] Irenaeus, *On Sole Sovereignty*, 5, 20, 5–6.

[24] Athanasius, *Discourses Against the Arians*, 2:70.

salvation. But Augustine also knew that, by virtue of that same unmerited grace, the Blessed Virgin Mary was preserved from sin —fourteen hundred years before Mary's Immaculate Conception was dogmatically defined by the Catholic Church:

> Having excepted the holy Virgin Mary, concerning whom, on account of the honor of the Lord, I wish to have absolutely no question when treating of sins—for how do we know what abundance of grace for the total overcoming of sin was conferred upon her, who merited to conceive and bear him in whom there was no sin? —so, I say, with the exception of the Virgin, if we could have gathered together all those holy men and women, when they were living here, and had asked them whether they were without sin, what do we suppose would have been their answer?[25]

In the same way, Hippolytus typifies this surprising (to an Evangelical) combination of biblical devotion, scorn for paganism, and typically Catholic language about Mary. Thus, on the one hand, Hippolytus writes a *Refutation of All Heresies* in which he heaps scorn on various forms of paganism, including the worship of the Great Mother and various other goddesses. But on the other hand, he's right at home seeing Mary as *Theotokos* as the fulfillment of biblical prophecy:

> [T]o all generations they [the prophets] have pictured forth the grandest subjects for contemplation and for action. Thus, too, they preached of the advent of God in the flesh to the world, his advent by the spotless and God-bearing [*Theotokos*] Mary in the way of birth and growth, and the manner of his life and conversation with men, and his manifestation by baptism, and the new birth that was to be to all men, and the regeneration by the laver [of baptism].[26]

And so, with the promulgation of the dogmas of Mary as *Theotokos* (A.D. 431) and Mary as Perpetual Virgin (A.D. 553), we arrive at

---

[25] Augustine, *Nature and Grace*, 36:42.
[26] Hippolytus, *Discourse on the End of the World*, 1.

a period in Church history that baffles even Miller and Samples, because even though these doctrines must—simply must—spring from "pagan soil," none of the acclaimed Christian writers of the era denied them and "nobody considered themselves pagan."[27]

Three Options

There are only three possible solutions to this puzzle. The first, which I was for several years, is to be so ignorant of what early Christians believed that you accept what "everybody knows." Then you simply parrot the claim that all the Mary stuff crept into the Church because, in the words of Ralph Woodrow's repudiated book, backsliding half-pagan Christians "reasoned that if people would be allowed to hold their ideas about a mother goddess, if this could be mixed into Christianity and the name Mary substituted, they could gain more converts." My problem was that I now knew that wasn't true.

The second option is to do what Miller and Samples have done: Look straight at this inconsistency, not know what to do with it, and go right on claiming Marian devotion springs from "pagan soil"—without providing a jot of evidence. The problem is that there is no evidence for this contention, since no Church Father ever appealed to any pagan source as the justification for Marian doctrine and devotion. On the contrary, they were insistent on studying "the Holy Scriptures, which are true and are of the Holy Spirit. You well know that nothing unjust or fraudulent is written in them."[28] Indeed, Irenaeus couples his warning against turning toward pagan gods with an admonition to remain faithful to Scripture:

> If, however, we are not able to find explanation for all those passages
> of Scripture which are investigated, we ought not on that account

---

[27] Miller and Samples, *The Cult of the Virgin*, 67.
[28] Clement, *Letter to the Corinthians*, 45, 1.

seek for another God besides him who exists. This would indeed be the greatest impiety. Things of that kind we must leave to God, the One who made us, knowing full well that the Scriptures are certainly perfect, since they were spoken by the Word of God and by his Spirit.[29]

So again and again, these same early Christians, who write in various tongues from various cultures and peoples in north, south, east, and west over a period of centuries, all agree on one thing: Their devotion to Mary comes, not from a longing to return to paganism, but from the apostles who handed on the Scriptures; therefore that devotion cannot conflict with Scriptures. That's why Justin Martyr does not appeal to pagan myth when he argues with a Jewish disputant named Trypho, but instead appeals to the book of Genesis in hailing Mary as the Second Eve, just as Irenaeus does:

Since we find it recorded in the memoirs of his apostles that he is the Son of God, and since we call him the Son, we have understood that he proceeded before all creatures from the Father by his power and will (for he is addressed in the writings of the prophets in one way or another as Wisdom, and the Day, and the East, and a Sword, and a Stone, and a Rod, and Jacob, and Israel); and that he became man by the Virgin, in order that the disobedience which proceeded from the serpent might receive its destruction in the same manner in which it derived its origin. For Eve, who was a virgin and undefiled, having conceived the word of the serpent, brought forth disobedience and death. But the Virgin Mary received faith and joy, when the angel Gabriel announced the good tidings to her that the Spirit of the Lord would come upon her, and the power of the Highest would overshadow her: wherefore also the Holy Thing begotten of her is the Son of God; and she replied, "Be it unto me according to thy word." And by her has he been born, to whom we have proved so many Scriptures refer, and by whom

---

[29] Irenaeus, *Adversus Haereses*, 2, 28, 2.

God destroys both the serpent and those angels and men who are like him; but works deliverance from death to those who repent of their wickedness and believe upon him.[30]

Likewise, the most strenuous defense of the Perpetual Virginity of Mary is made by the foremost biblical scholar of antiquity, Jerome, while Quodvultdeus of Carthage (a friend and disciple of Augustine's) is interested, not in Diana, Isis or Ashtoreth, but in Revelation 12 when he sees the cosmic and sinless figure of a glorious heavenly woman and tells us she

signifies Mary, who, being spotless, brought forth our spotless Head. Who herself also showed forth in herself a figure of holy Church, so that as she in bringing forth a Son remained a virgin, so the Church also should during the whole of time be bringing forth His members, and yet not lose her virgin estate.[31]

Similarly, Athanasius sees Mary's spiritual motherhood as the fulfillment, not of the cult of Isis, but of Jeremiah 31:22. And a growing flood of theologians in the early centuries of the Church see Mary prefigured, not by Venus, Athena, Hel, Eostre, Isis, Diana, Hera, and the like, but by Eve, Sarah, Deborah, Hannah, Judith, and Esther. For all these writers, the gaze is always firmly fixed on Scripture. It is not in Jason's Golden Fleece, but in Gideon's fleece wet with dew while all the ground beside had remained dry (Judges 6:37–38) that they see a type of Mary receiving in her womb the Word Incarnate yet remaining a Virgin.[32] It is from the Old Testament, not the works of Ovid or Homer that the Fathers derive images and titles of Mary such as:

---

[30] Justin Martyr, *Dialogue with Trypho*, 100.

[31] Quodvultdeus, *De Symbolo* 3, PL 40, 661.

[32] Cf. Ambrose, *de Spirit. Sanct.*, I, 8–9, *PL*, 41, 705; St. Jerome, Epist., cviii, 10; *PL*, 42, 886.

- The "Temple of God" She is the Holy of Holies in which God dwelt. (Ephraim the Syrian,[33] Jerome,[34] Ambrose[35])

- The "Rod of Jesse" from whom blossomed Christ (Ambrose,[36] Tertullian,[37] Jerome[38])

- The "East Gate" of the Temple spoken of by Ezekiel (Jerome[39])

- The "Ark of the Covenant" (Athanasius,[40] Gregory the Wonder-Worker[41])

- The "Staff of Aaron" (Ephraim the Syrian[42])

- The "Burning Bush that is Not Consumed" (Gregory of Nyssa[43])

Of course, many Evangelicals will contest the application of these various Old Testament texts to Mary. But that's getting ahead of ourselves. The question before us now is not "Did the Church Fathers misinterpret Scripture?" It is "Did the Church Fathers get their Marian theology and devotion from paganism?" And the simple answer to this question is that nowhere in the length and breadth of early Christian writings do you find an appeal to goddess worship, polytheism, the Great Mother, Venus, Athena, Diana, Ashtoreth, or anything else in pagan belief as the source for devotion to Mary as the sinless, perpetually-virgin *Theotokos*

---

[33] Ephraim the Syrian, *Praise of the Mother of God.*

[34] Jerome, *Against Helvidius*, 8.

[35] Ambrose, *On the Holy Spirit*, III, xi, 80.

[36] Ambrose, *In Luc.*, 2, 24.

[37] Tertullian, *Against the Jews*, 9, 26.

[38] Jerome, *Letter 22 to Eustochiam*, 19.

[39] Jerome, *Letter 48 to Pammachius*, 21.

[40] Athanasius, *Homily of the Papyrus of Turin.*

[41] Gregory the Wonder-Worker, *Homily on the Annunciation to the Holy Virgin Mary.*

[42] Ephraim the Syrian, *Hymn 1 on the Nativity.*

[43] Gregory of Nyssa, *The Life of Moses*, Book II.

who was assumed into Heaven. Instead, you find appeals to the teaching of the apostles and the witness of Holy Scripture.

It was this simple fact that compelled me to face the third option and realize that, despite what "everybody knew," I had never actually seen a shred of hard evidence that the early Church imported paganism into the gospel. Rather, the only "evidence" I had was that: a) my own Evangelical tradition found the feminine atmosphere of the Catholic faith strange; b) my first impressions of Marian devotion and doctrine had given me the creeps; c) I was unable to see the scriptural basis for most of Catholic Marian teaching and devotion, and; d) as a result, I had uncritically absorbed the basic Evangelical assumption that Catholic devotion to Mary "simply must" be pagan. So rather than keep a conclusion and continue searching for non-existent evidence to support it, I thought I'd look at the evidence and find out what conclusions it supported.

Which brings us, of course, to Christmas.

3

Reclaiming Creation for the Creator

The very thing which the Nature-religions are all about seems to have really happened once: but it happened in a circle where no trace of Nature-religion was present. It is as if you met the sea-serpent and found that it disbelieved in sea-serpents: as if history recorded a man who had done all the things attributed to Sir Launcelot but who had himself never apparently heard of chivalry. . . . Now if there is such a God and if He descends to rise again, then we can understand why Christ is at once so like the Corn-King and so silent about him. He is like the Corn-King because the Corn-King is a portrait of Him. The similarity is not in the least unreal or accidental. For the Corn-King is derived (through human imagination) from the facts of Nature, and the facts of Nature from her Creator; the Death and Re-birth pattern is in her because it was first in Him. On the other hand, elements of Nature-religion are strikingly absent from the teaching of Jesus and from the Judaic preparation which led up to it precisely because in them Nature's Original is manifesting itself. . . . Where the real God is present the shadows of that God do not appear; that which the shadows resembled does.

—C. S. Lewis[1]

Merry Christmas! Pull up a chair next to the Norse pagan Yule log on this cold winter solstice evening. Admire the German pagan Christmas tree and the way we've tastefully decked the halls with Druidic boughs of holly and mistletoe. While you're doing

---

[1] C. S. Lewis, *Miracles: A Preliminary Study* (New York: Macmillan, 1978), 114–16.

that I, with festal cheer, shall sip my Bailey's Irish Cream and tell you why the feast in which Mary plays the most prominent role of all—Christmas—turns out to have much less promise than meets the eye in supporting the claim that Christianity in general, and Marian Christianity in particular, is merely warmed-over paganism.

Pseudo-Knowledge and "Pagan Christmas"

Time was when I, like most people, took it for granted the winter solstice and, in particular, the Roman Feast of the Birth of the Unconquered Sun were simply pagan celebrations that survived into Christian times. In fact, when I set out to write this book I still thought this. But I discovered the reality is far more complicated and interesting. Indeed, it turns out this widely assumed "fact" that "everybody knows" is probably another sample of pseudo-knowledge. For according to William Tighe, a church history specialist at Pennsylvania's Muhlenberg College, "the pagan festival of the 'Birth of the Unconquered Sun' instituted by the Roman Emperor Aurelian on 25 December 274, was almost certainly an attempt to create a pagan alternative to a date that was already of some significance to Roman Christians. Thus the 'pagan origins of Christmas' is a myth without historical substance."[2]

The fact is, our records of a tradition associating Jesus' birth with December 25 are decades older than any records concerning a pagan feast on that day.

> [T]he definitive "Handbook of Biblical Chronology" by professor Jack Finegan (Hendrickson, 1998, revised edition) cites an important reference in the "Chronicle" written by Hippolytus of Rome three decades before Aurelian launched his festival. Hippolytus said

[2] William Tighe, "Calculating Christmas," *Touchstone*, December 2003. Available at http://touchstonemag.com/archives/article.php?id=16-10-012-v as of April 26, 2008.

Jesus' birth "took place eight days before the kalends of January," that is, Dec. 25.

Tighe said there's evidence that as early as the second and third centuries, Christians sought to fix the birth date to help determine the time of Jesus' death and resurrection for the liturgical calendar —long before Christmas also became a festival.[3]

In short, there was agitation in the early Church concerning not Jesus' birthday but the day upon which the historical Good Friday and Easter fell. In the Eastern Church, the tradition focused on April 6 as the date for the original Good Friday, while in the Western Church it was widely held that the date was March 25. Why does this matter? Tighe continues:

At this point, we have to introduce a belief that seems to have been widespread in Judaism at the time of Christ, but which, as it is nowhere taught in the Bible, has completely fallen from the awareness of Christians. The idea is that of the "integral age" of the great Jewish prophets: the idea that the prophets of Israel died on the same dates as their birth or conception.

This notion is a key factor in understanding how some early Christians came to believe that December 25th is the date of Christ's birth. The early Christians applied this idea to Jesus, so that March 25th and April 6th were not only the supposed dates of Christ's death, but of his conception or birth as well. There is some fleeting evidence that at least some first century and second century Christians thought of March 25th or April 6th as the date of Christ's birth, but rather quickly the assignment of March 25th as the date of Christ's conception prevailed.

It is to this day commemorated almost universally among Christians as the Feast of the Annunciation, when the Archangel Gabriel brought the good tidings of a savior to the Virgin Mary, upon whose acquiescence the Eternal Word of God ("Light of Light,

---

[3] Richard Ostling, "Why is Dec. 25 the date to celebrate Christmas? Two explanations compete," *North County Times*, December 24, 2004. Available at http://www.nctimes.com/articles/2004/12/23/special_reports/religion/21_50_1412_22_04.txt as of August 15, 2007.

True God of True God, begotten of the Father before all ages'')
forthwith became incarnate in her womb. What is the length of
pregnancy? Nine months. Add nine months to March 25th and you
get December 25th; add it to April 6th and you get January 6th.
December 25th is Christmas, and January 6th is Epiphany.[4]

And because these traditional, albeit competing, birth dates were
already being revered in the rapidly growing Church, the emperor
of a failing pagan empire instituted the Feast of the Unconquered
Sun not only as an "effort to use the winter solstice to make a political statement, but also almost certainly [as] an attempt to give
a pagan significance to a date already of importance to Roman
Christians."[5]

In addition to this there's another small but telling point. As
Richard Ostling reports, we also find that St. John Chrysostom
(a patriarch of Constantinople who died in A.D. 407) noted that
Christians had celebrated December 25 from the Church's early
days. Chrysostom reinforced his point with an argument that used
Scripture, not pagan mythology, for corroboration:

Luke 1 says Zechariah was performing priestly duty in the Temple
when an angel told his wife Elizabeth she would bear John the
Baptist. During the sixth month of Elizabeth's pregnancy, Mary
learned about her conception of Jesus and visited Elizabeth "with
haste."

The 24 classes of Jewish priests served one week in the Temple,
and Zechariah was in the eighth class. Rabbinical tradition fixed
the class on duty when the Temple was destroyed in A.D. 70 and,
calculating backward from that, Zechariah's class would have been
serving Oct. 2–9 in 5 B.C. So Mary's conception visit six months
later might have occurred the following March and Jesus' birth nine
months afterward.[6]

---

[4] Tighe, "Calculating Christmas."

[5] *Ibid.*

[6] Ostling, "Why is Dec. 25 the date to celebrate Christmas?"

So how did it become "common knowledge" that Christmas is really just a warmed-over pagan festival? It happened through a series of ironies capped by yet another example of pseudo-knowledge.

The first irony is the reaction of the Christians of the late Roman Empire to Aurelian's attempt to co-opt Christmas and make it a pagan day of celebration. Instead of fighting with Sun-worshippers who were trying to rip off their feast, early Christians simply "reappropriate[d] the pagan 'Birth of the Unconquered Sun' to refer, on the occasion of the birth of Christ, to the rising of the 'Sun of Salvation' or the 'Sun of Justice.'"[7] Mark that, because we shall return to it.

The next irony happens in the seventeenth and eighteenth centuries, when the myth of "pagan Christmas" really took hold.

> Paul Ernst Jablonski, a German Protestant, wished to show that the celebration of Christ's birth on December 25th was one of the many "paganizations" of Christianity that the Church of the fourth century embraced, as one of many "degenerations" that transformed pure apostolic Christianity into Catholicism. Dom Jean Hardouin, a Benedictine monk, tried to show that the Catholic Church adopted pagan festivals for Christian purposes without paganizing the Gospel.
>
> In the Julian calendar, created in 45 B.C. under Julius Caesar, the winter solstice fell on December 25th, and it therefore seemed obvious to Jablonski and Hardouin that the day must have had a pagan significance before it had a Christian one.[8]

Note that: Jablonski began, not with evidence, but with an assumption that the winter solstice must have had significance to Roman pagans before it had a Christian one. In other words, Jablonski simply noticed a correspondence between the Julian calendar's solstice and Christmas and assumed the pagan feast must have been the prior one even though he had no proof for his

---

[7] Tighe, "Calculating Christmas."

[8] *Ibid.*

theory. Meanwhile, Hardouin, rather than challenge that assumption, simply went along with it. And the entire myth about Christmas being a warmed-over pagan sun-worshipping feast is based upon the work of these two authors.

> But in fact, the date [December 25] had no religious significance in the Roman pagan festal calendar before Aurelian's time, nor did the cult of the sun play a prominent role in Rome before him.
>
> There were two temples of the sun in Rome, one of which (maintained by the clan into which Aurelian was born or adopted) celebrated its dedication festival on August 9th, the other of which celebrated its dedication festival on August 28th. But both of these cults fell into neglect in the second century, when eastern cults of the sun, such as Mithraism, began to win a following in Rome. And in any case, none of these cults, old or new, had festivals associated with solstices or equinoxes.[9]

What Can We Learn From This?

It is vital we not get bogged down in minutiae and miss the blazingly obvious. For instance, we must not get distracted by the irrelevant question of whether Roman Christians were right to place Jesus' birthday on December 25. Nor should we waste time saying, "Ah ha! Some early Christians relied on the unbiblical Jewish tradition of 'integral age' or Chrysostom's 'rabbinic tradition'!" Again, granted: the date of Christmas isn't found in Scripture. But that isn't what matters.

The crucial thing is not, "Did the early Christians get the date of Christmas right?" It is, rather, "What mattered to them as they determined the date of Christmas?" And when you look at that, you again immediately realize that what dominates their minds is not Diana, Isis, sun worship, or anything else in the pagan religious world. What interests them is—from our modern multicultural perspective—stunningly insular. Their debates are consumed not

---

[9] *Ibid.*

by longing for goddess worship, pagan mythology, or a desire to import Isis and Diana into the faith, but by the exact details of the New Testament record of Jesus' death, alloyed with a Jewish —not pagan—theory about when Jewish—not pagan—prophets die. The early Christians don't care a bit how pagan priests ordered their worship in the Temple of Diana at Ephesus. They care intensely about how Levitical priests ordered their worship in the Temple of Solomon at Jerusalem. These Christians are riveted on Scripture and the details of Jewish and Christian history and tradition. They don't give a hoot what sun worshipers, Osiris devotees, or Isis fans might think.

A Common Objection

At this point, someone might object, "But you yourself acknowledge that the early Christians reappropriated the pagan Birth of the Unconquered Sun to refer to the birth of Christ." True. I acknowledge that when Aurelian tried to co-opt a Christian holy day by designating it as the date for a pagan festival, Christians checkmated Aurelian by refusing to allow him to claim a sort of copyright on the sun for paganism. Instead, they insisted on returning the sun to the service of God its Creator—whom Scripture calls the True Light of the World, and a Sun, and a Shield— and did not make the blunder of worshipping the creature. They behaved rather like modern Christians who offer punning riffs on current cultural phenomena ("Jesus: He's the Real Thing," "Christ: Don't Leave Earth Without Him," etc.). Exactly what these Christians did not do was take passages of Scripture that referred to Jesus and apply them to Apollo or some other pagan deity. Nor did they look to any pagan deity to tell them about Jesus; they knew perfectly well that Jesus could be represented as the Sun of Justice and Light of the World long before Aurelian invented his pagan festival. That's because early Christians were behaving in a way perfectly consistent with Scripture, becoming "all things to all men" (1 Cor. 9:22), not "holding the form of religion while denying the power of it" (2 Tim. 3:5).

This matters immensely because it bears directly on the first moment the early Catholic Church really did borrow something from pagans. And not just any pagans, mind you, but actual adherents of Babylonian Mystery Religion. And most amazingly, the early Catholics' decision to do so receives the complete approval of, and even hearty defense by . . . Evangelicals.

We Three Kings of Orient Are / Astrologers Who Traverse Afar

As a young Evangelical, one of the things I routinely heard from critics of Christianity was that "everybody knows" the story of the Magi in Matthew 2 is a pious fiction invented by the Evangelist. Since Evangelicals take a very high view of Scripture and believe (like the Catholic Church) that "Scripture must be acknowledged as teaching solidly, faithfully and without error that truth which God wanted put into sacred writings for the sake of salvation,"[10] it mattered to me whether Scripture was preserving truth or was just a bunch of legends. And since my first investigation, subsequent reading has only added to my conviction that there are ample historical grounds for the story of the Magi.

First—and often overlooked by moderns who have an irrational prejudice against treating Scripture as one source of ancient historical testimony—is Matthew 2 itself, which says "wise men (Greek: *magoi*) from the East" appeared in Jerusalem one day, seeking "he who has been born king of the Jews." They claimed to have "seen his star in the East" and came to worship him. Matthew tells us they brought gold, frankincense, and myrrh as gifts and that their visit provoked the paranoid Herod to kill all the boys in Bethlehem under two years old. Matthew also notes

---

[10] *Dei Verbum*, 3, 11.

they returned to their own country in secret after having been warned in a dream not to return to Herod.

Not that there's no hint of legend attaching to the Magi, of course. Matthew doesn't tell us how many Magi there were, nor does he claim any of them were royalty. So how did they attain their legendary crowns and fixed number of three?

The number part is pretty easy: three gifts, three magi. As to their alleged royalty, this is more complicated. Beyond the biblical record, there's other evidence about them.[11] The historical *magoi* appear to have been a priestly caste in eastern lands. The Greek historian Herodotus tells us Magi were the sacred caste of the Medes.[12] And Jeremiah refers to one of these eastern priestly figures, a Nergal Sharezar, as *Rab-Mag*, "Chief Magus" (Jer. 39:3, 39:13). Magi had long been involved in the various religious and political struggles of Persia and their influence continued through the Assyrian, Babylonian, Persian, and Parthian empires. By the time of Jesus, they had long provided priests for Persia and been a major religious influence in the region. One ancient writer named Strabo says Magian priests formed one of the two councils of the Parthian Empire.[13]

Magoi is, of course, related to our English word "magic" but it's not really accurate to speak of Magi as "magicians." They lived in an age which hadn't yet distinguished between the attempt to understand and control nature by what we now call "science" and the attempt to understand and control nature by what we now call "magic." So we might say the Magi practiced the rudiments of astronomy and the rudiments of astrology.

Precisely what star they saw, and whether it was a natural or supernatural event, we do not know. We do know Jupiter conjoined Saturn three times in seven months in 7 B.C. We also know Mars

---

[11] Nicely summarized in the 1913 *Catholic Encyclopedia*. Available at http://oce.catholic.com/index.php?title=Magi as of August 18, 2008.

[12] Herodotus, *Histories*, I, 101.

[13] Strabo, *Geography*, 11, 9, 3.

joined them and produced a very striking configuration at about that time. Further, there's some speculation that the Star of Bethlehem may have been an occultation of Jupiter by the moon that occurred in 6 B.C., with the royal planet dramatically re-emerging from behind the moon. We even have an ancient Chinese chronicle, the *Ch'ien-han-shu*, which states that an object, probably a nova, or new star, was observed in March in 5 B.C. and remained visible for 70 days.[14]

Evangelicals who assume that any contact between biblical and pagan beliefs can only lead to corruption of biblical teaching should note that there's very good reason to think the Magi's beliefs were a mix of Persian astrology and messianic ideas floating around their country, courtesy of the significant Jewish population that had lived there since the days of Nebuchadnezzar, five centuries before. An American culture that's quite familiar with *Fiddler on the Roof* or the tales of Isaac Bashevis Singer should not marvel that, after 500 years, stories far more sacred to the Jews than these folk tales would be widely known among the educated elite in Persia. And a Magian knowledge of sacred Jewish texts certainly fits with Herod's behavior in slaughtering the innocents of Bethlehem.

Some critics have found this story of Herod's brutality absurd. Yet we know from non-biblical sources that Herod was indeed profoundly paranoid about rivals to his throne. He had his own children put to death to protect it (whereupon Augustus, who had granted Herod his puppet kingdom, remarked that since Herod observed kosher laws to placate his Jewish subjects, "It is better to be Herod's pig than Herod's son"[15]). But beyond this psychological evidence, there is in Scripture itself a tantalizing suggestion about why Herod would react so ferociously to the news of a

---

[14] For a thorough discussion of some of the possible astronomical phenomena that might underlie the story of the Star of Bethlehem, see Mark Kidger, *The Star of Bethlehem: An Astronomer's View*, (Princeton, N.J.: Princeton University Press, 1999).

[15] Macrobius, *Saturnalia*, 2:4:11.

newborn "king of the Jews"—a reason that dovetails remarkably well with what we know of the Magi.

You see, Herod—the "king of the Jews"—was not a Jew. He was an Edomite, or Idumaean, as they had become known by the time of Christ.[16] Edomites were descendants of Esau, Jacob's brother. Jacob, you will recall, received the blessing and birthright from Isaac that Esau was supposed to get (Gen. 27). From that time on, rivalry existed between the brothers (and their descendants).

Centuries after Jacob and Esau, when Israel escaped from Egypt and was journeying to the Promised Land, Moses requested passage through the land of the Moabites (a people closely allied with the Edomites) and was refused. In fact, the Moabites tried to destroy Israel. As part of their plan, the Moabite king, Balak, hired Balaam the prophet to curse Israel (Num. 22–24). However, as hard as Balaam tried, he found he could only bless the Chosen People.

What's significant about this is Balaam's third blessing on Israel. For he declared (in a prophecy that was, by Herod's time, widely regarded as messianic):

> I see him, but not now;
>   I behold him, but not nigh:
> *a star shall come forth out of Jacob,*
>   *and a scepter shall rise out of Israel;*
> it shall crush the forehead of Moab,
>   and break down all the sons of Sheth.
> *Edom shall be dispossessed,*
>   Seir also, his enemies, shall be dispossessed,
>   while Israel does valiantly.
> By Jacob shall dominion be exercised,
>   and the survivors of cities be destroyed!
>
>   (Num. 24:17–19; emphasis added)

---

[16] See, for instance, the 1913 *Catholic Encyclopedia* entry on Herod. Available at http://oce.catholic.com/index.php?title=Herod as of August 18, 2008.

"Edom shall be dispossessed" by a "star . . . out of Jacob." Would a paranoid Edomite king with Herod's psychological track record be unnerved by the Magi's report of a star and their question, "Where is he who has been born king of the Jews?"? Would such a king, who had proved himself willing to murder his own son to protect his throne, hesitate to slaughter the children of nameless peasants in an obscure village if he thought it would keep him from being "dispossessed"? To paraphrase Augustus, in such a situation, it would be better to be Herod's pig than Herod's subject.

So it turns out there's good reason, both biblical and extra-biblical, to think that—in an age especially inclined to look for signs and portents in stars and holy books—Persian astrologers would have seen such signs and portents in the skies and sacred books of Israel and Herod would have acted upon them.

Other biblical figures make the same kind of connections. In Revelation 4 and 5 we meet the "four living creatures"—angelic beings John describes as looking like a lion, an ox, a man, and an eagle. These images, in turn, refer us back to the vision of Ezekiel 1, in which the prophet (in exile in Babylon some six centuries before John) sees an identical vision. But there's also strong evidence to link these four images to the constellations of the zodiac.[17] For the biblical writers indicate a high degree of familiarity with the constellations, with the exception that Scorpio was probably known to them as the Eagle. The four cherubim mentioned in Revelation 4:6–7 are very likely the middle signs in the four quarters of the zodiac: The lion is Leo, the ox is Taurus, the man is Aquarius, and the eagle corresponds to Scorpio. John lists them in counter-clockwise order, backward around the zodiac.

---

[17] For a full discussion of John's use of zodiac imagery, see Austin Marsden Farrer, *A Rebirth of Images: The Making of St. John's Apocalypse* (Albany, N.Y.: State University of New York Press, 1986). Also see David Chilton, *The Days of Vengeance: An Exposition of the Book of Revelation* (Fort Worth, Tex.: Dominion, 1990), 158–59.

This is not, however, an example of star worship on John's part any more than Matthew's gospel is a tribute to Babylonian astrology. Rather, it's just another example of the common biblical understanding that the heavens, like all the rest of creation, are a sign made by God and pointing to God. In the words of Psalm 19:1, "The heavens declare the glory of God." To the people of biblical times, the stars' groupings are not random, for the simple reason that nothing in creation is random. Rather, they thought the macrocosm of creation showed the glory of God writ large across the heavens just as the microcosm of the tabernacle (and, later, the temple) showed it on a smaller, more intimate scale.[18]

So it should be no surprise to us that John's star imagery borrows not from paganism but from Jewish Scripture. For in the Old Testament (cf. Num. 2), the arrangement of the twelve tribes of Israel around the tabernacle probably corresponded to the zodiac and its twelve signs.[19] In fact, at least six ancient synagogues (at Hammat Tiberias, Beit Alpha, Huseifa, Susiya, Naaran, and Sepphoris) are decorated with the zodiac.[20] The hope of the twelve tribes of the Chosen People is that Israel is the beginning of the new order of things, whose destiny and divine authorship is symbolized by the twelve constellations. Indeed, the link between the "heavenly host" ruled by Yahweh Sabaoth (the "Lord of Hosts") and the nation of Israel is very strong, for the heavenly host, or army of angelic powers symbolized by the stars, is ruled over by the very same God who commands the armies of Israel or the "earthly

---

[18] For a fuller discussion of the relationship between cosmos and temple, see Joshua Berman, *The Temple: Its Meaning and Symbolism Then and Now* (Northvale, N.J.: Jason Aronson, 1995), 10–14.

[19] Michel Barnouin, "*Remarques sur les tableaux numériques du Livre des Nombres,*" RB 76 (1969) 351–64. Michel Barnouin, "*Les recensements du Livre des Nombres et l'astronomie babylonienne,*" VT 27 (1977), 280–303.

[20] Prof. Rachel Hachlili, "Mosaic Floors in Ancient Synagogues," *Jewish Heritage Online Magazine.* Available at http://www.jhom.com/topics/stones/mosaic.html as of August 15, 2007.

host." The earthly tabernacle was understood by Israelites to be a miniature of God's heavenly dwelling. Both were attended by the armies of the Lord, composed of the angels and the people of Israel.

So the Jews spoke of the earth as having four corners (Rev. 7:1), not because they thought the earth was square, but because the altars in the tabernacle and the temple had four corners—and they regarded the earth as a gigantic altar, just as they thought of the temple as a miniature cosmos. Similarly, in Genesis 37:9, Jacob and his family are likened to the sun, moon, and twelve stars. The book of Judges also reflects the notion that the "heavenly host" of God and the earthly host of Israel are all members of the army of God. That's why Judges 5:20 celebrates the defeat of Jabin and his general Sisera by singing, "From heaven fought the stars, from their courses they fought against Sisera." John, like Matthew, stands firmly in a Jewish and biblical stream of thought, even as he ponders images of Persian astrology.

What the Church Does and Does Not Learn From the Magi

This brings us back to the main issue. One curious thing to note about these scriptural treatments of Magian astrology is where they do not lead us. Contrary to what Dan Brown, Alexander Hislop and Tim LaHaye contend, they do not result in a "hybrid" religion where pseudo-Christian Catholics worshiped stars or goddesses. Matthew doesn't leave us with the idea that we ought to practice the religion of Babylonian astrologers, and, as we have seen, John's gaze is fixed firmly on Genesis, Numbers, Ezekiel, and the God those Jewish holy books proclaim.

But at the same time, unlike many Evangelicals, the authors of Scripture also do not conclude that every contact between biblical faith and paganism can only result in the corruption of Christianity. Instead Matthew, John, and the Catholic Church after them take a very sensible third way. To the Evangelical afraid of defilement by any contact with pagan Babylonian astrology, the evangelists say, "The Magi were right to think there was something connecting all of creation. Our own fathers recognized the same and reflected it in their inspired writings. So God met the Magi where they were, just as he met our fathers where they were, and worked within their limitations to lead them to Bethlehem."

But to the pagan-minded like Dan Brown, who tries to claim Christianity is just warmed-over Babylonian astrology, the Church also insists the astrologers were wrong about what kind of connection exists between Heaven and earth. It is not the stars connecting creation: it's the Creator himself. Heaven and earth meet when God becomes human in Jesus Christ, not when Jupiter aligns with Mars. So, says the Church, for the Magi (or more to the point, anyone) to go back to astrology after finding Jesus would be like going back to stand at the road sign instead of going on to the destination to which the sign points. Once God has given you himself, turning back to astrology or anything else is like opting to go back to the miserable mud hut you came from in the broken-down ox cart you came in, while God stands there holding out a credit card, the keys to a Maserati with a full gas tank, and a floor plan of the gorgeous estate he wants you to have. Like all sin, that choice requires a whole lot of stupidity.

That's why Matthew records how the Magi brought the best they had to the Christ Child and then "fell down and worshipped him" (Matt. 2:11). The Magi didn't stand gawking at the astrological road sign; they found and worshipped the Christ it signified. And the Church likewise quickly saw in them an image, not of Babylonian Mystery Religion, but of repentance and completion—a turning away from what was false in their pagan beliefs and a confirmation of what was true. The Magi make a sacrificial offering of the best they had to offer, not to Babylonian deities, but to the newborn King of the Jews. Indeed, in these offerings, the Church sees the truth of Jesus himself: gold for his kingship, frankincense for his priesthood, and myrrh for his burial.

Note the curious spiritual jiu-jitsu at work here. The scriptural pattern never takes biblical forms and fills them with pagan substance. It sees pagan life as a confused mixture of human thought and imagination, demonic deception, and divinely-led intuition. Thus, where necessary, the Church upbraids paganism for worshipping the creature instead of the Creator but, where possible, she affirms the human wisdom of Aristotle and Plato, honors the ordinary feasts and fasts of the peasant, and appropriates some pagan forms if she can fill them with Christian substance and thereby reclaim the creature for the proper service of the Creator.

Paul and Paganism

The same pattern can be seen in the life and works of the apostle Paul. Like many Evangelicals, Paul sometimes chastises paganism for its folly and darkness. For instance, in his most famous diagnosis of the ills of the pagan world, he writes:

> For the wrath of God is revealed from heaven against all ungodliness and wickedness of men who by their wickedness suppress the truth. For what can be known about God is plain to them, because God has shown it to them. Ever since the creation of the world his invisible nature, namely, his eternal power and deity, has been clearly perceived in the things that have been made. So they are without excuse; for although they knew God they did not honor him as God or give thanks to him, but they became futile in their thinking and their senseless minds were darkened. Claiming to be wise, they became fools, and exchanged the glory of the immortal God for images resembling mortal man or birds or animals or reptiles.
>
> Therefore God gave them up in the lusts of their hearts to impurity, to the dishonoring of their bodies among themselves, because they exchanged the truth about God for a lie and worshipped and served the creature rather than the Creator, who is blessed for ever! Amen.

For this reason God gave them up to dishonorable passions. Their women exchanged natural relations for unnatural, and the men likewise gave up natural relations with women and were consumed with passion for one another, men committing shameless acts with men and receiving in their own persons the due penalty for their error.

And since they did not see fit to acknowledge God, God gave them up to a base mind and to improper conduct. They were filled with all manner of wickedness, evil, covetousness, malice. Full of envy, murder, strife, deceit, malignity, they are gossips, slanderers, haters of God, insolent, haughty, boastful, inventors of evil, disobedient to parents, foolish, faithless, heartless, ruthless. Though they know God's decree that those who do such things deserve to die, they not only do them but approve those who practice them (Rom. 1:18–32).

Therefore, he warns the Ephesians:

Now this I affirm and testify in the Lord, that you must no longer live as the Gentiles do, in the futility of their minds; they are darkened in their understanding, alienated from the life of God because of the ignorance that is in them, due to their hardness of heart; they have become callous and have given themselves up to licentiousness, greedy to practice every kind of uncleanness (Eph. 4:17–19).

Some modern readers, finding it hard to believe in the supernatural, are inclined to read Paul as though he sees nothing in the pagan world besides corruption and licentious fantasies. But this is to misread him. For though Paul denies that pagan deities such as Zeus, Athena, and Apollo exist, he also warns that there is nonetheless a spiritual creature at work behind the idol.

What do I imply then? That food offered to idols is anything, or that an idol is anything? No, I imply that what pagans sacrifice they offer to demons and not to God (1 Cor. 10:19–20).

That is, the sacrifices offered to the idol are, whether we hairless bipeds realize it or not, offered to demons: superhuman angelic spirits that have rebelled against God and seek to destroy us in their pride and malice. Evangelicals are very sanely alive to this reality, while our present age—blinded by both atheism and neo-paganism—is insensible to it.

That said, it must also be noted that there's another aspect to Paul's thought about paganism that isn't as commonly known. Paul showed us this side of his thinking on the day he was, to his great embarrassment, declared a pagan god by a rabble at Lystra:

> Now at Lystra there was a man sitting, who could not use his feet; he was a cripple from birth, who had never walked. He listened to Paul speaking; and Paul, looking intently at him and seeing that he had faith to be made well, said in a loud voice, "Stand upright on your feet." And he sprang up and walked. And when the crowds saw what Paul had done, they lifted up their voices, saying in Lycaonian, "The gods have come down to us in the likeness of men!" Barnabas they called Zeus, and Paul, because he was the chief speaker, they called Hermes. And the priest of Zeus, whose temple was in front of the city, brought oxen and garlands to the gates and wanted to offer sacrifice with the people (Acts 14:8–13).

As we would expect, Paul and Barnabas do not respond by saying, "Okay, folks, in a spirit of multiculturalism, let's worship Zeus and Hermes, too." Instead, "they tore their garments and rushed out among the multitude, crying, 'Men, why are you doing this? We also are men, of like nature with you, and bring you good news, that you should turn from these vain things to a living God who made the heaven and the earth and the sea and all that is in them'" (Acts 14:14–15).

But then Paul adds something startling to those who think Christianity is simply hostile to everything in pagan life. He declares, "In past generations he allowed all the nations to walk in their own ways; *yet he did not leave himself without witness*, for he did good and gave you from heaven rains and fruitful seasons, satisfying your hearts with food and gladness" (Acts 14:16–17; emphasis added). In saying God did not "leave himself without witness" among the pagans, Paul is teaching that paganism, whether at Lystra or among the Magi, included muddled but real insights into the One God of Israel who has revealed himself fully in Jesus

Christ, and that the time had now come for pagans to recognize that all that was good and true in their own culture was owed, not to the religious illusions they had pursued until then, but solely to the God of Israel who had revealed himself fully in Christ.

Paul didn't believe pagans were dead wrong about absolutely everything, just as he didn't say "What we need is some Zeus and Hermes worship to make this Jesus sect more attractive to Gentiles." Instead, when he came to Athens and found a people fascinated by myths, mysteries, and pagan rites, he said:

> Men of Athens, I perceive that in every way you are very religious. For as I passed along, and observed the objects of your worship, I found also an altar with this inscription, "To an unknown god." What therefore you worship as unknown, this I proclaim to you. The God who made the world and everything in it, being Lord of heaven and earth, does not live in shrines made by man, nor is he served by human hands, as though he needed anything, since he himself gives to all men life and breath and everything. And he made from one every nation of men to live on all the face of the earth, having determined allotted periods and the boundaries of their habitation, that they should seek God, in the hope that they might feel after him and find him. Yet he is not far from each one of us, for
>
> "In him we live and move and have our being"; as even some of your poets have said,
>
> "For we are indeed his offspring."
>
> Being then God's offspring, we ought not to think that the Deity is like gold, or silver, or stone, a representation by the art and imagination of man. The times of ignorance God overlooked, but now he commands all men everywhere to repent, because he has fixed a day on which he will judge the world in righteousness by a man whom he has appointed, and of this he has given assurance to all men by raising him from the dead (Acts 17:22–31).

Paul cites not the Old Testament but Greek poets as he argues that Jesus is the One the Greeks had rightly been looking for in all the wrong places. Paul isn't creating a "hybrid religion." He's not telling the Athenians that their poets and monuments to the "unknown god" are things Christianity needs in order to complete or understand itself. Rather, Paul is establishing what will become a time-tested method of Christian evangelism: taking some aspect of pagan religion or culture and, if it can be done without diluting the gospel, referring it to Christ. That's because Christ is the author of all creation and therefore imparts to creation signs that point us toward him as we attempt to "feel after him and find him."

What Hunger Is For

Which brings us back to Christmas, as well as every other bit of pre-Christian paganism—Easter bunnies, halos, you name it—that Christianity has used to serve the Christian message.

For here again both Dan Brown and Evangelical critics of Catholic Marian doctrine and devotion make similar arguments about the alleged pagan origins of Christianity. So, for instance, Brown declares it significant that Christian halos in art resemble Egyptian sun disks,[21] as though the association of luminosity and divinity could only occur to an Egyptian and must be stolen by Christians. But this is like saying that Paul stole the idea of walking around on two legs from Aristotle, or that Jesus borrowed the notion of eating supper with his friends from Socrates.

What all these "strange coincidence" theories ignore is that some religious ideas are as universal as broad daylight. That's why a Hebrew psalmist could describe the Lord God as a sun and a shield (Ps. 84:11) while Greeks could associate divine splendor with the sun in the figure of Apollo, Pharaoh Akhnaton could mistake the sun for God, and Jesus could call himself the Light of the World (cf. John 8:12). It's just not that hard to associate light that illumines the eye with truth that illumines the mind. Every normal human makes that association, including atheistic philoso-

---

[21] Brown, *The Da Vinci Code*, 232.

phers of the eighteenth century who proclaimed themselves "Enlightened" while refusing to worship Ra, Apollo, or Jesus Christ.

It's not strange, therefore, to see Christian evangelists employing such obvious motifs to express life in Jesus Christ. What would be very strange—even incomprehensible—is if Christians had not done this. Christianity teaches its followers that there is one God, the author of all truth, beauty, and goodness. It would be passing strange if a Christian who truly believed this were to encounter the truths in Aristotelian philosophy, the beauties in Egyptian art, or the goodness of sunlight and then refuse to allow anything about them into Christian life on the grounds that doing so would corrupt Christianity. One may as well argue that a modern minister must worship Greek gods if he illustrates a sermon with one of *Aesop's Fables*.

All this is fairly obvious. But when we turn from Jesus to Mary and Google "Virgin Mary" and "Isis," we discover that (among the 92,000 sites which hold forth on this topic as of this writing) pseudo-knowledge dominates the field. For example, as the result of our Google search, we learn from the Metropolitan Museum of Art that, "A mother figure is a central object of worship in several religions (for example, images of the Virgin and Child call to mind Egyptian representations of Isis nursing her son Horus)."[22] Well, sort of, but that's not telling us anything useful about Christianity. The issue here isn't whether we can draw similarities between Isis nursing Horus and Mary nursing Jesus. The issue is whether we must conclude that the story of Jesus and Mary would not exist without Egyptian religion. That's because any image of a mother nursing her child calls to mind Isis nursing Horus, and Mary nursing Jesus or—for that matter—Lara nursing Kal-El, the infant Superman, on the planet Krypton. The immemorial image of Mother and Child is one of the enduring realities of the human race. So why should such imagery not impress Christian minds?

---

[22] Available at http://www.metmuseum.org/toah/hd/virg/hd_virg.htm as of August 15, 2007.

And if the pagan imagery is older than Christianity, how could Christians fail to make imagery that resembles it, given the limited number of ways to portray a mother and child? Put another way, if we think we should reject Mary's presence in Catholic Christianity because a mother figure is central to many pagan religions, why shouldn't we also reject the presence of Jesus, the Bible, and ministry in Evangelical Christianity because a god figure, sacred texts, and spiritual leaders are central in many pagan religions?

What all this "Christianity is pagan" business tells us is that the fallacy of the undivided middle—where any similarity is taken to prove identity, as in "dogs have four legs, tables have four legs, therefore dogs are tables"—is alive and well and living in pseudo-knowledgeland. The fallacy works so long as no one notices that Christianity has always filled pagan forms with Christian content and has never filled Christian forms with pagan content. If we never notice that, then we miss the fallacy at work, not only in *The Da Vinci Code*, but in the typical Evangelical case against the "pagan Catholic Mary."

If we're going to avoid this fallacy, it won't be enough for us to prove that something in the faith resembles something in paganism or vice versa. If one is really to make the case that a Christian doctrine is just warmed-over paganism, you must establish that something Jesus taught has been destroyed and replaced with pagan substance. If that can't be shown or, more potently, if it can be shown that some pagan form has been filled with Christian content, then so far from showing that Christianity is really pagan, we have instead shown that something in paganism is an anticipation of the fullness of Christian revelation.

So, for instance, when we look at the Christmas carol, "The Holly and the Ivy," a disciple of Brown can't argue that "It's really just a celebration of warmed-over Druidic religion, since holly and ivy were plants sacred to Druids." For the song does not refer us to pagan gods. It refers us to the gospel:

The holly bears a blossom,
As white as lily flow'r,
And Mary bore sweet Jesus Christ,
To be our dear Saviour:

The holly bears a berry,
As red as any blood,
And Mary bore sweet Jesus Christ,
To do poor sinners good.

In short, just as the apostles focus the Star of the Magi and the monument to the unknown god on Christ and not on Apollo or Zeus, so the song takes these relics of Druidic belief and focuses them on Jesus, their true object, and not on some Celtic or Germanic deity. Dittos with stuff like Christmas trees. Precisely what irks a neo-pagan is that a tree spirit or Mother Earth is not the object of worship at Christmas. Rather, Christianity has restored the tree to the service of its Creator by using it to remind us of the Messianic Branch who springs from the Root of Jesse (cf. Is. 11). Neo-pagans are irritated, not gratified, by the fact that "Eostre" eggs have become symbols, not of Eostre or some other fertility deity, but of the empty tomb of Jesus Christ.

This pattern of reclaiming creation for the Creator continues throughout Christianity right into the present. A few years ago, in my hometown of Seattle, there was a weird sort of New Age neo-pagan nightclub called "The Sanctuary" that took over an abandoned church building. It was, as you might guess, rather thin on theology, and rather long on prostitution, drugs, and underworld sleaze with minors. But for a while they tried to play the neo-pagan card with big signs on the side of the building that read "We are Children of the Universe! We have a right to be here!" (This was in response to various complaints and police investigations.) Eventually, the place got raided and shut down. Not long after that, a non-denominational church group bought the place and turned it into a real sanctuary devoted to the worship of the Father, Son, and Holy Spirit.

That kind of reclamation happens all through Christian history. It's why St. Peter's Square in Rome has an Egyptian obelisk with a crucifix atop it and it's why there's a Church in Rome, known as "Santa Maria Sopra Minerva" (Saint Mary Above Minerva), built on the ruins of a shrine to the goddess Minerva. Neither of these places symbolize that the Catholic faith is dedicated to the worship of Egyptian gods or that Minerva is now being worshipped under the guise of Mary. Rather, they symbolize that the Christian faith has not only the form of godliness but also the power thereof, and that power means the power to seize spiritual strongholds, overthrow them, and use their high places to worship the God of Abraham, Isaac, and Jacob rather than the false idols of paganism. Rather than adopt a "scorched earth" policy toward things and places that have been defiled by idolatry, the Christian instinct has always been to offer the defiled thing back to God who makes all things clean.

For the earth is the Lord's and everything in it (Ps. 24:1). So, as C. S. Lewis says, the pagan nature god "is derived (through human imagination) from the facts of Nature, and the facts of Nature from her Creator; the Death and Re-birth pattern is in her because it was first in Him." So when a pagan myth speaks of a dying god who comes back to life (like, say, Osiris), or when a pagan sees something important in the relationship of mother and child (like Isis and Horus) or notices a relationship between physical light and spiritual enlightenment (like haloes and sun disks), the sensible response is that this is what we ought to expect, just as the sensible response to a tasty dinner is, "That's what hunger is for." After all, if the Christian revelation is true and therefore truly fulfills the deepest longings of the human soul, then we would expect pre-Christian culture to anticipate Jesus, desire him, and have flashes of insight about him. So we should not be surprised if some pre-Christian myths give us dim and fleeting glimpses of him, just as we should not be surprised that they're also distorted and ultimately unhealthy, because they were born within a fallen race that was, as Paul says, "feeling after him" yet also living in the darkness of sin.

But what we must notice most of all is how little this pre-Christian paganism was of interest to the early Church. As Lewis noted, when you finally meet a character in history who acts like the dying and rising god of the nature religions, he comes from a Jewish tradition that has no interest in nature religions. He's the sea serpent who doesn't believe in sea serpents. And his early followers are like him; their focus is almost entirely on Jewish Scripture and almost never on pagan religious texts. They notice Jewish feasts like Passover, Pentecost and Hanukkah, never pagan ones. They honor only the God of Israel, and spurn the idols of pagans as demons. They set the dates of their feasts not according to the solstices but according to internal squabbles over their own holy books. And when they do come face-to-face with paganism, they never import pagan substance into the Christian form. Instead, they always, where possible, fill the pagan form with Christian content, thereby reclaiming creation for the Creator.

And what applies in all this to our Lord also applies to our Lady. For the Catholic Church derives none of her Marian doctrines from paganism, but sees Mary, as much as Jesus, reflected in the text of Holy Scripture. The problem is that Evangelicals don't always read Scripture the way the apostles did. And that, as we shall see, makes all the difference in the world as we turn our attention to the only Marian doctrine that Catholics and Evangelicals agree about—the Virgin Birth of Christ.

4

Reading Scripture as the Apostles Did

To me, though I am the very least of all the saints, this grace was given, to preach to the Gentiles the unsearchable riches of Christ, and to make all men see what is the plan of the mystery hidden for ages in God who created all things; that through the church the manifold wisdom of God might now be made known to the principalities and powers in the Heavenly places.

—Ephesians 3:8–10

Poor Matthew! His gospel seems a favorite target for critics of the faith. If it's not somebody complaining about the Magi, it's one of those "Mysteries of the Bible" shows on TV. A friend of mine caught one of them a few years ago. It featured a couple of theologians eager for their fifteen minutes of fame. So rather than talking about the faith, they obligingly told the camera that Jesus was not born of a virgin. They supported their claim by alleging that Matthew misunderstood the prophet Isaiah.

The story is this: the Hebrew Bible (known to Christians as the Old Testament) was translated into Greek a few centuries after Isaiah's time. This Greek translation is called the Septuagint. In the original Hebrew text of Isaiah 7:14, we read that an "*almah* shall conceive and bear a son, and shall call his name 'Immanu-el.'" *Almah* means "young woman" and refers to any young woman, virgin or not. But when the Septuagint's Jewish translators rendered Isaiah into Greek, they didn't translate *almah* as "young woman." They rendered the word into Greek as *parthenos*, which means "virgin." About two centuries later, when Matthew wrote his life of Christ, he used this Greek translation when declaring of the Virgin Birth, "All this took place to fulfil what the Lord had spoken by the prophet: 'Behold, a virgin shall conceive and bear a son, and his name shall be called Emmanuel' " (Matt. 1:22–23). Thus, said the TV theologians, we now know Matthew was wrong to believe in the Virgin Birth because Isaiah did not say "virgin" but "young woman."

As a result, my friend was wrestling with what seemed an inevitable set of conclusions: a) the Septuagint translation of Isaiah 7:14 is flat wrong; b) Matthew was ignorant of the actual meaning of Isaiah 7:14; c) Matthew therefore derived his belief in Jesus' Virgin Birth from a wrong translation of Isaiah; and d) the Church thus erred in defining her dogma of the Virgin Birth of Christ. However, this enters into a whole complex of mistakes, not clarifications. To find out what's really going on, let's look again at the New Testament use of Old Testament Scripture.

Prophecy, Not Prediction

It is easy for the modern reader, who usually begins with the notion that the Church is "based on the Bible," to adopt a kind of "checklist" view of Old Testament prophecy, as though every first century Jew had an agreed-upon set of "Old Testament Messianic Verses" against which all messianic claimants were measured. Indeed, many Christian apologetics books today lay out precisely this sort of checklist:

Prophecy:	Source:	Fulfillment:
The Messiah must . . .	O.T.	N.T.
Be born in Bethlehem	Mic. 5:1–2	Mt. 2:1, Lk. 2:4–7
Be adored by great persons	Ps. 72:10–11	Mt. 2:1–11
Be sold for 30 pieces of silver	Zech. 11:12	Mt. 26:15

One could easily get the impression that all a first century Jew had to do was follow Jesus around and tick off prophecy fulfillments on his Old Testament Messianic Prophecy Checklist and he ought to have known everything Jesus was going to do before he ever did it.

But as Augustine once observed, the Bible's messianic prophecies were not so much revealed by the Old Testament as they were hidden there. This isn't a notion cooked up in the Dark Ages to justify reading into the Old Testament whatever Christians wanted to see there. It's a truth taught to the apostles themselves by the risen Christ:

> Then he said to them, "These are my words which I spoke to you, while I was still with you, that everything written about me in the law of Moses and the prophets and the psalms must be fulfilled." Then he opened their minds to understand the scriptures, and said to them, "Thus it is written, that the Christ should suffer and on the third day rise from the dead, and that repentance and forgiveness of sins should be preached in his name to all nations, beginning from Jerusalem" (Luke 24:44–47).

In short, "Moses and all the prophets" had written "concerning himself" (Luke 24:26–27), according to the risen Jesus. It is from Jesus, then, that the apostles get the idea that the whole life and ministry of Christ fulfilled the Scriptures. But Jesus fulfills them not by ticking off items on a Messianic Prediction Checklist compiled in the Old Testament but by revealing the gospel that was hidden there.

This is why Paul says the New Covenant was "veiled" until the gospel took away the veil (cf. 2 Cor. 3:14). It's also why he declares that the gospel was "*not made known* to the sons of men in other generations as it has now been revealed to his holy apostles and prophets by the Spirit" (Eph. 3:5; emphasis added). Paul insists the deepest meaning of the Old Testament was seen only after the life, death, and resurrection of Christ.

Because the New Covenant is hidden, not revealed, in the Old Testament, nobody before the time of Jesus says, "Why, it's plain from Scripture the Messiah will be born of a virgin, be raised in Nazareth, be rejected by the chief priests, be handed over to Gentiles, be crucified with thieves, rise from the dead, ascend into Heaven, and abrogate the circumcision demand for Gentiles as he breaks down the barriers between man and woman, slave and free, Jew and Gentile." Even the disciples themselves, close as they were to Jesus, didn't anticipate the Crucifixion, much less the Resurrection—even when Jesus rubbed their noses in messianic prophecy (cf. Mark 9:9–10). As John says, they did not understand from Scripture that the Messiah had to rise from the dead, even while they were standing in the very mouth of Jesus' empty tomb, gawking at his grave clothes (cf. John 20:1–10). And yet, these same apostles later speak of the Resurrection—like the Virgin Birth—as a fulfillment of Old Testament prophecy. What do they mean if the Old Testament prophecies aren't predictions upon which everybody based their understanding of Messiah?

They mean Christ fulfilled, brought to fruition, and was the ultimate expression of the same revelation toward which all the Old Testament was straining and pointing. They mean Jesus was the One to whom the Law and the prophets were directed by the Holy Spirit, even when the sacred writers themselves did not know all that their words pointed toward (cf. 1 Pet. 1:10–11).

This is why the early Church was never troubled by an issue that often vexes modern minds: namely, why the New Testament often appears to take Old Testament texts out of their immediate context and read them as commentaries on Christ. For the early Church doesn't see the Old Testament as talking about something different from Christ, but rather sees it in relationship to him. What appear to the modern mind as separate themes and events in the Old Testament appear to the New Testament writers as so many spokes on a wheel, all connected to the Hub who is Christ.

For instance, Hebrews 2:13 applies Isaiah 8:18 to Christ: "Here I am, and the children God has given me." In its original context, Isaiah is speaking about himself and his disciples. He's not offering a prediction that the coming Messiah would say this. Yet the author of Hebrews sees Christ, far more than Isaiah, fulfilling the text. Why? Because Christ and his Church are, most fully, what Isaiah and his disciples were in a kind of foreshadow.

Isaiah's words, like all words, are signs signifying something: in this case Isaiah and his own disciples. But Isaiah and his disciples are, in their turn, also signs signifying something even greater: Christ and his disciples. For Christ and his Church are the same thing Isaiah and his disciples were: "signs and portents in Israel from the Lord of hosts, who dwells on Mount Zion" (Is. 8:18). Isaiah and his disciples fulfill the passage in an immediate sense. But the early Church saw no particular reason why the God Isaiah worshiped couldn't fulfill it even more profoundly when he became incarnate and established his Church. So the author of Hebrews, reading the Isaian passage with hindsight illumined by Jesus' entire life and ministry, hears the Composer of the Symphony of Divine Revelation play a theme through Isaiah and his disciples in a minor key which he will ultimately play in a major key in Christ.

The same thing applies to Isaiah 7:14, the passage Matthew quotes with regard to Jesus' Virgin Birth. Matthew knew his Bible extremely well and was perfectly aware that this passage had an immediate fulfillment in Isaiah's day. Isaiah's Emmanuel Prophecy comes in an hour of national crisis during the reign of Ahaz, one of the lousier kings of Judah descended from David. In Isaiah's day, the people of Israel had actually been split into two realms: a northern kingdom called "Israel" and a southern kingdom called "Judah." At the time of the Emmanuel prophecy, Israel has formed an alliance with pagan Syria against Ahaz's kingdom of Judah. As a result the people of Judah are in a muck sweat about the future of their country. So Isaiah goes to Ahaz and tells him not to worry about the alliance because God will take care of Judah. To back up his assurances, Isaiah offers Ahaz the chance to "ask a sign of the LORD your God" (Is. 7:11). Ahaz, jerk that he is, refuses. He pretends he's too pious to put God to the test, but actually he does not want to obey Isaiah because he'd rather put his faith in practical politics and not in Isaiah's mystical hocus-pocus.

It is then the Immanu-el Prophecy is given: "Behold, an *almah* shall conceive and bear [or "is with child and shall bear"] a son, and shall call his name Immanu-el" [which, as Matthew will later note, means "God with us"]. What does Isaiah mean?

Most immediately, Isaiah means Ahaz will have a son—Hezekiah —who will carry on the line of David so that, as Nathan had long ago prophesied to David, "your throne shall be established forever" (2 Sam. 7:16).[1] In other words, Isaiah is telling Ahaz that "God is with" the Davidic throne of Judah still and his kingdom will therefore not be defeated by the menacing alliance to the north. And that's what happened. The alliance against Judah fails and Hezekiah is born. The prophecy's most immediate sense is indeed fulfilled, not by a virgin birth, but by the *almah* or wife of Ahaz and the birth of a new "son of David" to carry on the Davidic line.

But there remains in pre-Christian Jewish tradition a persistent belief in larger and second meanings in its Bible. As the centuries roll on there is, for instance, a growing sense among the Jews that Nathan's prophecy to David of an everlasting throne recorded in 2 Samuel 7 (despite these immediate fulfillments) speaks not so much of an everlasting political rule, but of some higher and greater Throne yet to come. And so, when the political power of David's house actually does fail, Israel reflects on Nathan's words and wonders what deeper meaning might be in them. Indeed, Isaiah himself tells Israel that from the "stump of Jesse" (that is, the fallen Davidic dynasty which loses power during the Babylonian Captivity in the fifth century B.C.), a "shoot" shall grow. Of this coming king, this "Son of David," this Anointed One or Messiah Isaiah prophesies:

> And the Spirit of the LORD shall rest upon him, the spirit of wisdom and understanding, the spirit of counsel and might, the spirit of knowledge and the fear of the LORD. And his delight shall be in the fear of the LORD (Is. 11:2–3).

---

[1] For a good argument that Isaiah's prophecy is immediately fulfilled by the birth of Hezekiah, see Rev. William G. Most, "The Problem of Isaiah 7:14," *Faith and Reason*, Summer 1992. Available at http://www.ewtn.com/library/ SCRIPTUR/FR92203.TXT as of August 15, 2007.

In other words, Isaiah is aware the story does not end with the birth of Hezekiah. The Lord saves Ahaz' throne, not for Ahaz' sake, nor for Hezekiah's, but for the sake of the promise given long ago to David that will only be finally fulfilled when the ultimate Son of David is born, the Son of whom Isaiah also spoke:

> For to us a child is born, to us a son is given; and the government will be upon his shoulder, and his name will be called "Wonderful Counselor, Mighty God, Everlasting Father, Prince of Peace." Of the increase of his government and of peace there will be no end, upon the throne of David, and over his kingdom, to establish it, and to uphold it with justice and with righteousness from this time forth and for evermore (Is. 9:6–7).

So the birth of a son of David named Hezekiah both fulfills the prophecy of Isaiah 7:14 and foreshadows an even greater fulfillment in the birth of the ultimate Son of David, Jesus.

This idea of immediate and long-term fulfillment of prophecy is found throughout Scripture and the New Testament simply assumes that we know this. For instance, Moses tells Israel to await a prophet like him (cf. Deut. 18:15) and indeed many prophets like Moses appear. That's why we have the books of Isaiah, Jeremiah, Ezekiel and the rest. Yet instead of seeing them as the final fulfillment of Moses' promise, Israel instead believes some ultimate prophet is also coming; an Anointed One, Servant, Prophet, Son of David, or Son of Man (these titles are all used in the Old Testament), a man who will "utter what has been hidden since the foundation of the world" (Matt. 13:35), a man of whom all the Old Testament prophets—including Moses—are dim foreshadowers. This is why the Jews asked John the Baptist if he was "*the* prophet" (John 1:21; emphasis added).

Understanding of the Old Testament's messianic message was characterized by clarity and obscurity in the time of Christ. Certain texts (like Nathan's prophecy of an everlasting Davidic throne) were clearly understood by most first century Jews to be messianic. But other passages were overlooked entirely until Jesus' astounding life put them into proper context. Nobody

knew beforehand that Psalms 69 and 109[2] prophesied the election
of Matthias to the apostolic office forfeited by Judas; or understood the Passover lamb's unbroken bones as a prophetic image
of Christ's unbroken bones (cf. John 19:31–36, Ex. 12:46 and
Num. 9:12); or saw in advance that Isaiah 53 bears witness to the
Crucifixion and Resurrection. If they had, says Paul, they would
never have crucified the Lord of Glory (1 Cor. 2:8). All these
things are only seen after the fact to be eerily prophetic of Christ
and his Church. They fill out the rough picture sketched by the
more widely-acknowledged messianic prophecies, but only after
Jesus' life has provided the key to understand them.

The early Christians were very well aware of this immedi-
ate/remote, hidden/clear character of the Hebrew Bible. So they
never mistook the Old Testament for a handy-dandy Rolodex filled
with prediction proof texts and neatly organized by category to
form the basis of Jesus' ministry. The early Christians saw the Old
Testament bearing inspired witness to the extraordinary man who
had dwelt among them; that is, they put Scripture in the witness
box, not on the judge's bench.

So they did not, for instance, read "Zeal for thy house will con-
sume me" in Psalm 69 and then decide "Let's make up a story
about Jesus cleansing the Temple based on this verse." On the
contrary, to their great surprise, Jesus cleanses the temple (John
2:13–16) and then his disciples remember the psalm and are struck
by how it fits the event (cf. John 2:17).

This happens again and again in the New Testament. The disciples are as surprised as anybody else when Jesus heals the sick
or raises the dead. They don't foresee Christ's miracles by reading the Old Testament. Rather, the ministry of Christ happens
to them like a bolt from the blue and they then see an uncanny
connection between what Jesus does and the weird way that it fits

---

[2] The Septuagint renderings of Psalm 69:25 ("Let his habitation become
desolate, / and let there be no one to live in it.") and Psalm 109:8 ("His office
let another take.") are cited by St. Peter in Acts 1:20.

the Old Testament. When Jesus is sold for thirty pieces of silver or his hands and feet are pierced on the cross, the apostles do not discover this fact by sticking their noses into Zechariah 11:12–13[3] or Psalm 22:16.[4] Rather, after Jesus is raised, they remember these things were written and, blinking their eyes in amazement, exclaim, "It was staring us in the face all along and we didn't see it!" The Old Testament is not the basis of their belief in these things; it's the witness to the truth of what they've already seen.

And so, back to my friend's worries about the Virgin Birth. First off, the Septuagint's translators didn't make a "wrong" translation of *almah* into *parthenos*. Recall that the translation was made quite a bit before the sexual revolution in the 1960s (in fact, two centuries before Christ). Hence, it was commonly assumed in the culture of the translators that a newly married young woman would naturally be a virgin. Faced with a choice between the Greek word for "young woman" and the Greek word for "virgin" they opted, in the Providence of God, to use the latter.

Second, whatever may have been the reason for the Septuagint's choice of words, Matthew did not, in any event, derive his belief in Mary's virginity from Isaiah 7:14. He didn't sit down one day, read the Septuagint version of Isaiah, and say to himself, "Let's see. Isaiah says something about a virgin here. So if I'm going to cook up a Christ figure, I'd better make him the son of a virgin so it'll fit with this text."

On the contrary, the only reason the apostles are telling stories about Jesus at all is not because they saw Jesus' birth, but because they saw the Risen Jesus. It was this that got their attention and

---

[3] "Then I said to them, 'If it seems right to you, give me my wages; but if not, keep them.' And they weighed out as my wages thirty shekels of silver. Then the LORD said to me, 'Cast it into the treasury'—the lordly price at which I was paid off by them. So I took the thirty shekels of silver and cast them into the treasury in the house of the LORD."

[4] "Yea, dogs are round about me; / a company of evildoers encircle me; / they have pierced my hands and feet."

prompted them to inquire about his origins. And they inquired about Jesus' origins, not from Isaiah, but from the only person who could have told them the story: Mary.

It is only after they've heard Jesus tell them the Law and the prophets are, ultimately, about him, and only after they've heard the story of Jesus' birth from Mary that they look at their Septuagint Bibles, find Isaiah's prophecy and see Jesus reflected in it. The Church's faith in the virginity of Mary does not originate in some textual gaffe, but in the historical fact of the Virgin Birth of Christ related by Mary, a fact to which the Septuagint translation bears providential witness. The basis of the Church's faith, then as now, is Jesus Christ himself.

The Spiritual Sense of Scripture

There are even more interesting things to note about this profoundly biblical way of reading Scripture. The first is that Matthew, like all the New Testament authors and even Jesus himself, sees more than one "sense" at work in Scripture. That is, they take seriously the literal sense of the Old Testament, but they also take that literal sense for granted and see behind it, not another meaning but a deeper meaning. They believe the stories reported there as fact are true, but they also believe these things "were written down for our instruction, upon whom the end of the ages has come" (1 Cor. 10:11). So they read (and teach their disciples to read) the Old Testament as packed with all sorts of secondary meanings pointing to Jesus and his Church.

That's why Jesus, taking for granted the literal sense of Exodus 16's story of the manna in the wilderness, nonetheless sees in the manna an image of himself, the Bread of Life (John 6:31–35). It's why Paul, likewise taking for granted Israel's passage through the Red Sea as historical, also sees it as an image of baptism (1 Cor.

10:1–2). It's why John the Baptist sees the Passover lamb as a foreshadow of Jesus (John 1:29). Again and again, the New Testament reads the Old Testament this way.

As with Jesus, So with Mary

But that pattern does not stop with applications to Jesus. The apostles also see the Church and the saints foreshadowed in the Old Testament as well. In Romans 8:36, for instance, Paul looks at Psalm 44, which was written as a lament for the sufferings of Israel in a time of national disaster, and sees in the innocent suffering of the psalmist a foreshadow of the innocent sufferings of persecuted Christians. Likewise, Peter takes the description of Israel as a "kingdom of priests and a holy nation" (Ex. 19:6) and applies it to the Church (cf. 1 Pet. 2:9), since he regards the Church as the New Israel.

In exactly the same way, Luke subtly but clearly likens Mary to the ark of the covenant, the holiest object in the Old Testament and, by a powerful use of allusion, he drives the point home to his audience.

What is "allusion"? It's a passing reference made to something so familiar that an audience will immediately recognize it without long, tedious explanations. So, for instance, if I look at my eldest son, Luke, breathe heavily, and say in a deep and ominous voice, "Luke! I am your father!" I instantly call to his mind, not just one line, but the entire *Star Wars* saga. Everybody knows what I'm alluding to. Similarly, when Matthew cited Isaiah's Emmanuel prophecy he is alluding, not merely to one line out of Isaiah, but ultimately to the whole story of the everlasting throne promised to David by God. All this was, to Matthew's readers, as familiar as *Star Wars* is to us. For nothing was more familiar to the first Christians than the Old Testament.

So when Luke records the story of the Annunciation and Mary's visit to Elizabeth, he's assuming we will get his allusions to ark-related events in the Old Testament. That's why, when he records the words of the archangel that the Holy Spirit will "overshadow" Mary (Luke 1:35), he uses the exact Greek word used in the Septuagint to describe the way the *Shekinah*—the very glory of God—"overshadowed" the place where the ark was kept (cf. Ex. 40:35; 1 Kgs. 8:10). It's also why Luke notes that both David and Elizabeth use the same language to greet the old and new arks:

> And David was afraid of the LORD that day; and he said, "How can the ark of the Lord come to me?" (2 Sam. 6:9).

> And why is this granted me, that the mother of my Lord should come to me? (Luke 1:43).

In 2 Samuel, we're told "David *arose and went*" to the hill country of Judah, "to bring up from there the ark of God" (2 Sam. 6:2; emphasis added). We also read:

> And the ark of the LORD remained in the house of O'bed-e'dom the Gittite *three months*; and the LORD blessed O'bed-e'dom and all his household (2 Sam. 6:11; emphasis added).

Not accidentally, Luke notes that Mary "*arose and went* to the hill country of Judah" (Luke 1:39) where she remained with Elizabeth for "three months" (Luke 1:56; emphasis added).

Finally, David brought the ark back to Jerusalem, his new capital. As he led a procession back into the city, he was "leaping and dancing before the LORD" (2 Sam. 6:16).

And again, not accidentally, Luke 1:41 records that, "when Elizabeth heard the greeting of Mary, the babe leaped in her womb; and Elizabeth was filled with the Holy Spirit."

To a reader immersed in the Old Testament, these connections between Mary and the ark are plain as day. And when you think about it, it's not surprising they were seen, given that the tabernacle which held the ark was the dwelling place of God in the Old Covenant and, as John tells us "the Word became flesh and [in literal Greek] tabernacled among us" (John 1:14). After all, what goes together with the Old Testament ark that resided in the tabernacle?: the rod of Aaron the High Priest, the Ten Words of the Law, and manna (Heb. 9:4). So, likewise, Mary's womb contained the High Priest of the New Covenant, who is the Word made flesh and the Bread of Life.

Not surprisingly then, John also sees the same connection between Mary and the ark of the covenant when he announces in his Revelation:

> Then God's temple in heaven was opened, and the ark of his covenant was seen within his temple; and there were flashes of lightning, voices, peals of thunder, an earthquake, and heavy hail. And a great portent appeared in heaven, a woman clothed with the sun, with the moon under her feet, and on her head a crown of twelve stars; she was with child and she cried out in her pangs of birth, in anguish for delivery (Rev. 11:19–12:2).

Note how the imagery runs together, and remember that the chapter and verse breaks we're used to didn't exist in John's day. The Holy Spirit guides John's vision easily and naturally from the image of the ark to the image of the woman—a woman he goes on to describe as giving birth to a male child who rules the nations with a rod of iron and who is almost devoured by a great red dragon at his birth.

Now, in my early years as an Evangelical, I noticed that many of my fellow Evangelicals found it remarkably easy to detect bar codes, Soviet helicopters, Saddam Hussein, and the European Common Market encoded in John's Revelation. But when Catholics suggested that the glorious woman of Revelation might have something to do with the ark of the covenant, and that both might have something to do with the Blessed Virgin occupying a place of cosmic importance in the grand scheme of things, this was ridiculed as a preposterous distortion of the text. That's because, as I was taught, "everybody knew" that the woman of Revelation was really Israel, not Mary:

> This passage does not support the bodily assumption of Mary for several reasons. First, the "woman" does not represent Mary but

the nation of Israel for whom there is "a place prepared by God, that there she might be taken care of for twelve hundred and sixty days" (v. 6) during the tribulation period before Christ returns to earth (cf. Rev. 11:2–3).[5]

Or else "everybody knew" that the woman was really the Church, not Israel or Mary:

> Who is the woman in Revelation Chapter 12? The vast majority of Roman Catholics today will tell you, "Well, that's Mary." Who was she to the early church? Have you ever looked? In the early fathers, the Blessed Virgin, the Immaculate Virgin, is always the church, not Mary.[6]

Yet when I got past what "everybody knew" and actually looked at what the Fathers like Quodvultdeus of Carthage said I discovered something very different:

> The Woman signifies Mary, who, being spotless, brought forth our spotless Head. Who herself also showed forth in herself a figure of holy Church, so that as she in bringing forth a Son remained a Virgin, so the Church also should during the whole of time be bringing forth His members, and yet not lose her virgin estate.[7]

Likewise, Oecumenius writes:

> "And a sign appeared in heaven, a woman clothed with the sun and the moon was under her feet." As we said, it is speaking about the mother of our Savior. The vision appropriately depicts her as in heaven and not on the earth, for she is pure in soul and body, equal to an angel and a citizen of heaven. She possesses God who rests

---

[5] Norman Geisler and Ralph E. MacKenzie, *Roman Catholics and Evangelicals: Agreements and Differences* (Grand Rapids, Mich.: Baker Books, 1995), 313–14.

[6] James White, transcript of first of four seven-minute rebuttals from "Gerry Matatics vs. James White: Does the Bible Teach Sola Scriptura?" (November 1992, Omaha, Neb.). Available at http://vintage.aomin.org/1White07.html as of August 18, 2008.

[7] Quodvultdeus, *De Symbolo* 3, PL 40, 661.

in heaven—"for heaven is my throne"—it says yet she is flesh, although she has nothing in common with the earth nor is there any evil in her. Rather, she is exalted, wholly worthy of heaven, even though she possesses our human nature and substance. For the Virgin is consubstantial with us.[8]

Moreover, Ambrose summarizes the classic vision of the Fathers when, so far from pitting Mary against the People of God, he tells us that she is the "type of the Church."[9]

Indeed, the more I looked at the way that the early Church read her Bible, the sillier I was starting to feel. For I realized I was actually saying,

"A Jewish girl who stood at the pinnacle of the Old Covenant, summed up the entirety of Israel's mission and bore the One called the Son of the Most High, to whom the Lord God gave the throne of his father David promising 'he will reign over the house of Jacob for ever; and of his kingdom there will be no end' (Luke 1:32–33) —what could she possibly have to do with those images in Revelation 12 of a woman who gives birth to a male child who will rule the nations with a rod of iron? What flight of fancy could ever propose some likeness between the red dragon attempting to devour the woman's child and the attempt on the life of Jesus by Herod the Edomite, who comes from a people whose very name means 'red'? What remote similarity could there be between the image of the child snatched up to heaven and the Ascension of Christ, or the woman's flight from the jaws of a red dragon and the Holy Family's flight from Herod? Mary who said, 'Behold, I am the handmaid of the Lord; let it be to me according to your word' —what implausible connection could she ever have to the image of a mother whose offspring 'keep the commandments of God and bear testimony to Jesus'? (Rev. 12:17). How could anyone possibly see a parallel between a mother whose soul would be pierced by a sword (cf. Luke 2:35) and a woman suffering the birth pangs of the coming kingdom (cf. Matt. 24:8; Rev. 12:2)? Why, to grant such

---

[8] Oecumenius, *Commentary on the Apocalypse*, 12.1–2.

[9] Ambrose, *Expos. Lc.* II, 7: *PL* 15, 1555.

connections would be to suggest Mary was the Virgin Daughter of Zion, the Flower of her People, the Model Disciple, the Icon of the Church, the Mother of Sorrows, the Mother of Jesus and of all those united with him by faith and . . ."

Hmmm . . . er . . .

Yes, Scripture was looking rather Catholic at that.

In short, it began to look quite plausible to me that, rather than forcing us into an either/or choice between Mary, the Daughter of Zion, or the Church, the image of the woman in Revelation encompasses all these realities—just as Catholic teaching about Mary does. This is why the woman is portrayed as wearing "a crown of twelve stars." For just as the ark is an image of Mary, so Mary herself is a kind of image, summing up in herself the "Virgin Daughter of Zion" and standing, in a unique way, as a sign of all of Old Testament Israel. She is crowned with twelve stars because, in her, all the twelve tribes who have awaited the coming Messiah are summarized and perfectly represented. And, as she represents in her person the Virgin Daughter of Israel, so her son Jesus perfectly sums up in his person all the "sons of David" who have gone before him. Even more, just as the male child and the woman stand as symbols not only of Jesus and Mary, of the son of David and the Virgin Daughter of Zion, so they also point forward to the Church—that is, to the "rest of her offspring," the "brethren" who share in the sufferings of Christ.

For the same reason, the red dragon also has layers of meaning. Partly, as we have noted, he's very likely an allusion to Herod the Great, who, like the dragon, tried to "devour her child when she brought it forth" (Rev. 12:4). But beyond this, the dragon probably refers to the whole Herodian dynasty consisting, in total, of seven kings—"seven heads" (Rev. 12:3). The Herodians, remember, were not Jews but Edomites. They were, if you like, a kind of satanic counterfeit of the Davidic dynasty put on the throne not by God but by the Caesars (probably represented by the "ten horns" of power on the seven heads.) [10]

---

[10] Scott Hahn, in his audiocassette series "The End: A Study of the Book of

But beyond all of this, as Scripture shows, there is an even deeper layer of meaning to the dragon. For as the woman images Mary, and Mary images Israel and the Church, so the dragon images not only Herod and the Herodian dynasty in their wicked counterfeit of the house of David, but the ultimate source of the evil that seeks to destroy the male child, the woman and all they represent: "that ancient serpent, who is called the Devil and Satan, the deceiver of the whole world" (Rev. 12:9). This is why Revelation 12 alludes not only to Herod's attempt on Jesus' life and the slaughter of the innocents, but to all the sufferings of the Church ("the brethren"), of ancient Israel during the sojourn in Egypt and the wilderness (Revelation 12:14), and of mankind brought on by the "ancient serpent" who deceived the first Eve but who was defeated by the "seed of the woman," the new Eve.

And so Revelation 12 goes on to describe the battle with the Dragon as ultimately being fought not by human agencies but by supernatural ones. The archangel Michael serves as a kind of heavenly general in the war on the dragon (Revelation 12:7–8). Meanwhile, the "brethren" (i.e., those who are united with Christ and are numbered among the "rest of the offspring" of the woman) "conquered" the Dragon, not by force of arms, but by martyrdom, "by the blood of the Lamb and by the word of their testimony, they loved not their lives even unto death" (Rev. 12:11).

Two Important Conclusions

This multi-layered way of looking at not only Scripture, but the things which Scripture relates can be discussed at great length.[11] However, rather than multiply examples of this, suffice it to note two things here.

Revelation" (West Covina, Calif.: St. Joseph Communications) argues that the ten horns represent the ten Caesars from the founding of the Roman Empire to the destruction of Jerusalem in A.D. 70.

[11] And have been discussed in my book *Making Senses Out of Scripture: Reading the Bible as the First Christians Did* (Rancho Santa Fe, Calif.: Basilica, 1999).

The first thing is that Mary's relationship to the ark of the covenant is an example of the early Church seeing Mary, not from a pagan perspective, but from the perspective of an apostolic Tradition that is both written and unwritten. Devotees of the "Pagan Mary" theory completely ignore the fact that Mary is likened to the ark of the covenant, not to Pandora's Box, Artemis' quiver of arrows, Ishtar's purse, or Semiramis' knitting bag. The biblical writers, like the Fathers after them, have hearts, minds, and imaginations completely dominated by imagery from Scripture, not pagan myth. Indeed, so thoroughly are their minds focused on Jewish Scripture and apostolic Tradition that they simply assume that, as a baptized Christian, your mind will be focused that way too. That's why Luke does not explicitly write "Mary is the ark of the New Covenant" but instead expects us to connect the dots in what is, to him, a blazingly obvious allusion. In the same way, John does not laboriously spell out the obvious connection between the ark, the woman, Mary, the Virgin Daughter of Zion, and the Church. He also expects that we'll immediately and easily do it ourselves in light of apostolic Tradition and realize that this is what Scripture is reflecting.

In short, John and Luke are thinking like Catholics, not like Evangelicals. Or, to put it another way, the Catholic Church thinks like John, Luke, and the other New Testament authors—which is why the Church now teaches what she does about Mary just as she now teaches what she does about Christ.

5

Of Mustard Seeds and Mustard Plants

The kingdom of heaven is like a grain of mustard seed which a man took and sowed in his field; it is the smallest of all seeds, but when it has grown it is the greatest of shrubs and becomes a tree, so that the birds of the air come and make nests in its branches.

—Matthew 13:31–32

Of course, with a brassy statement like the one that ended the previous chapter, my Evangelical friends instantly encounter a difficulty. On the one hand, we have this portrait of a conservative early Church whose Tradition comes from the apostles. On the other hand, the modern Catholic Church appears to Evangelicals (as it long appeared to me) to add novel doctrines to the faith in broad daylight while claiming that they had been there all along.

So the exasperated Evangelical naturally cries out, "If these Marian doctrines come from the apostles as you claim, then where the blazes is the Immaculate Conception of Mary in Scripture and why did it not become dogma until 1854?! How come the Assumption isn't a dogma till 1950 if it's always been part of apostolic teaching?"

Barking Up the Wrong Tree: False Ideas of Sacred Tradition and the "Hidden Church"

These are, of course, very reasonable questions. And when the Church replies, at the Council of Trent, that Catholic "truth and teaching are contained in written books and in the unwritten traditions the apostles received from Christ himself or that were handed on, as it were from hand to hand, from the apostles under the inspiration of the Holy Spirit, and so have come down to us"[1] this doesn't seem at first like a very good answer. To Evangelicals, it looks as though the Church is basically saying, "Okay, so the Immaculate Conception isn't in Scripture. It's in, uh . . . Tradition! Yeah! That's the ticket! Tradition! St. Peter and the apostles used to talk about the Immaculate Conception and Assumption of Mary in exactly the same language Catholics do today. But the apostles kept it hushed up among themselves and left it out of the Bible till people were ready to hear it. So these doctrines always have been in Tradition because . . . uh . . . they were passed on at the Double-Secret Tradition-Passing-On Ceremony that all Catholic bishops have to go through in the dungeons beneath the Vatican! Then, when the time was ripe the Church told the rest of the faithful about them."

In other words, there is broad assumption among Evangelicals that what Catholics mean by sacred Tradition is a body of revelation that's secret, separate from, and parallel to Scripture, transmitted from bishop to bishop ("Psst! Mary is Immaculate, Ever-Virgin and Assumed into Heaven, pass it on!"), and then "leaked" into official teaching over the centuries. That is one reason why, not to put too fine a point on it, the Catholic appeal to Tradition smells like a rat to the "Bible-only" nose. Confronted with the baffling discovery of an early Church that looks pretty Catholic and a modern Catholic Church riddled with what appear to be teachings completely disconnected from Scripture, some Evangelicals seize on this misconception of sacred Tradition as the solution to their confusion. To explain the survival of "true Christianity" through the long ages when the Catholic Church was the only game in town, they will often posit a theory of the "hidden, true Church of Bible Christians" that allegedly rejected this false "sacred Tra-

---

[1] Council of Trent, *Decree on Sacred Scripture and Tradition*, Denzinger 783 (1501).

dition" and was, as a result, driven underground by a mass apostasy of proto-Catholics occurring shortly after the apostolic era. Supposedly, this hidden church of underground believers preserved the true biblical gospel through the long night of pre-Reformation error in which the "apostate" proto-Catholics evolved into full-blown Catholics and dominated the written record of Christianity with all those documents filled with sacred Tradition. Meanwhile, according to this theory, the true Bible Christians hid out in the hills or the catacombs as the Catholic Church made war on them. It is, so the theory goes, the documents of the fallen-away apostates we're reading when we read the works of writers like Clement of Rome, Ignatius, Irenaeus, Polycarp, Hippolytus, Athanasius, Augustine and all the other Fathers who make the early Church look so Catholic. Not until the Reformation was it safe for true Bible Christians to come out of hiding.[2]

The irony of the "hidden church" theory is that it requires the very idea it tries to refute, namely the absurd belief in a revelation secret, separate from, and parallel to Scripture. For, despite all her faults and failings, we at least know what the supposedly apostate Catholic Church was doing for fifteen centuries before the alleged hidden Christians allegedly emerged from the shadows and declared themselves to be Protestants. In addition to dealing with the inevitable sins of her fallen human members, the Catholic Church was busy defending the integrity of Sacred Scripture from heretics like Marcion; settling questions like "Is God a Trinity?"; withstanding the onslaughts of Islamic *jihads* and Viking longboats; laying the foundations for the rule of law amidst the chaos of the Dark Ages; converting nation after nation to Christ; integrating Scripture into all her worship and prayer; renewing art, science and philosophy; inspiring saints such as Augustine, Thomas Aquinas and Francis of Assisi; building hospitals

---

[2] For a fairly typical exposition of the "hidden church" theory, see J. M. Carroll, *The Trail of Blood* (Lexington, Ky.: Ashland Avenue Baptist Church, 1974).

and universities; and evangelizing the New World. In short, the Catholic Church was working tirelessly to do the things commanded by the Gospel of Jesus Christ.

Meanwhile, if any church lived a secret, separate, and parallel existence, it's the supposed "hidden church" which, for fifteen centuries, was so hidden that it did nothing, said nothing, accomplished nothing, and was so invisible that we do not even find a record of opposition to it by the supposedly apostate Catholic Church which allegedly usurped its place the moment the apostle John died. Some advocates of the "hidden church" theory will claim that various early heresies opposed by the Church were actually these hidden Bible Christians. The problem with this claim is that every heretical sect from A.D. 100 to A.D. 1500 teaches things a modern Protestant would not be especially eager to touch with a barge pole, such as the rejection of the Old Testament, the doctrine that the God of Israel is evil, and rejection of the Incarnation.

So if we want to argue that all record of the hidden church was obliterated by sinister Catholics, we'll have to ignore the mysterious fact that it's only the hidden church that seems to have been written out of the historical records. All the other groups the Catholic Church opposed (e.g., Gnostics, Arians, Sabellians, Manicheans, Modalists, Paulicians, Bogomils, Albigensians and a host of other movements) show up again and again in the polemical writings of the Church as movements to beware of—and with ample record of what they actually taught. Only the hidden church is completely absent from the historical record. And yet devotees of the "hidden church" theory expect us to think this was the Church whose light so shone that men praised their Father in heaven? This is the city on the hill that cannot be hid? This is the light of Christ burning for all the nations to see?

It's pretty obvious then that the "hidden church" theory is neither biblical, nor very good history, nor common sense. Indeed, it looks like nothing so much as the equally illusory cult of the Sacred Feminine that Jesus supposedly bequeathed to Mary Magdalene. Once again, there's no there there.

So is there another way to account for the apparent contradiction of an extremely Catholic-looking early Church whose Tradition never changes and a modern Catholic Church that seems to have changed a great deal from the early Church?

What Sacred Tradition Really Is

To answer that, we need to first ask, "Is sacred Tradition really a revelation secret, separate from, and parallel to Scripture?" The answer of the Catholic Church is "No. Indeed, it's precisely this view of Tradition which the Church has always condemned." That's because the notion that salvation lies in some secret knowledge given only to the elite is the essence of gnosticism, not Christianity. And the Catholic Church has always been gnosticism's mortal foe. That is why Irenaeus writes the following in the second century:

> It is within the power of all, therefore, in every Church, who may wish to see the truth, to contemplate clearly the tradition of the apostles manifested throughout the whole world; and we are in a position to reckon up those who were by the apostles instituted bishops in the Churches, and to demonstrate the succession of these men to our own times; those who neither taught nor knew of anything like what these heretics rave about. For if the apostles had known hidden mysteries, which they were in the habit of imparting to "the perfect" apart and privily from the rest, they would have delivered them expressly to those to whom they were also committing the Churches themselves. For they were desirous that these men should be very perfect and blameless in all things, whom also they were leaving behind as their successors, delivering up their own place of government to these men. . . .[3]

Irenaeus firmly commits the idea of "secret revelations" to the realm of heresy, and yet does so in the name of Scripture and

---

[3] Irenaeus, *Adversus Haereses*, 3, 3, 1.

sacred Tradition handed down from the apostles. So, if sacred Tradition is not a body of secret revelation, separate from and parallel to Scripture, from which the Church can suddenly produce brand-new dogmas like rabbits from a hat, what is it?

It is the living, growing truth of Christ passed down in the Church in both written and unwritten form in the common doctrine, common life, and common worship of the Church. Vatican II sums up the idea of Tradition by saying, "the Church, in her doctrine, life and worship, perpetuates and transmits to every generation all that she herself is, all that she believes."[4]

The common doctrine, life and worship of the Church can be seen in Acts 2:42 when the disciples devote themselves, not only to Bible study, but the fullness of the apostolic Tradition, described by Luke as "the apostles' teaching and fellowship . . . the breaking of bread and the prayers." The "apostles' teaching" is given, as Paul says, both by word of mouth and by letter (2 Thess. 2:15). In its unwritten form Tradition is not secret, separate from, and parallel to Scripture, but common, widely known, derived from the apostles (not from paganism) and—mark this—reflected in Scripture.

The "fellowship" and "the breaking of bread and the prayers" spoken of in Scripture means more than chummy glad-handing and church socials. The early Christians "devoted themselves" to the common life ("fellowship") and to the common eucharistic, liturgical worship of the Church ("the breaking of bread and the prayers")—a life and worship that's essentially public and communal, not private and esoteric. And just as it is for the Catholic Church today, the common teaching, life and worship of the Church in the New Testament is a living thing—a truth which was planted as a mustard seed in first-century Jerusalem and which has not ceased growing—just as our Lord prophesied in Mark 4:30–32. The mustard plant may not look like its seed anymore, but it is, if anything, more mustardy than ever. Just as

---

[4] *Dei Verbum*, 8, 1.

every branch and flower shooting out of the plant is in the seed, so every dogmatic development that shoots out of the Church was in the seed of apostolic Tradition handed down to us in written (i.e. Scriptural) and unwritten form.

It's this relationship between written and unwritten apostolic Tradition that lets the Church know, for example, that while Holy Communion is to be celebrated continually, the washing of feet is not, even though both actions were part of the Last Supper and even though in both cases Jesus commanded his disciples to imitate him. On the basis of the scriptural texts, read alone and without Tradition, we're powerless to make such a distinction. But since the Church has a common apostolic Tradition about how to read Scripture's accounts of the Last Supper, the Church was able to make this distinction.

In the same way, both Catholics and Protestants know how to contract a valid marriage, not because Scripture gives us any guidelines on how to do this, but because they're both the inheritors of sacred Tradition, which guides both groups in such matters. Catholics receive this Tradition from the apostles, preserved by the body of Christ in union with the bishops and Pope in succession from the apostles. Protestants receive pieces of this Tradition as part of the Christian heritage they took with them in the break with the Catholic communion. But in both cases, what we're looking at is Christians living by and developing sacred Tradition, not the letter of Scripture alone.

Similarly, both Catholics and Evangelicals reject polygamy, despite the fact that (as Martin Luther[5] and John Milton[6] both point

---

[5] Martin Luther, *De Wette*, II, 459. "I confess that I cannot forbid a person to marry several wives, for it does not contradict the Scripture. If a man wishes to marry more than one wife he should be asked whether he is satisfied in his conscience that he may do so in accordance with the word of God. In such a case the civil authority has nothing to do in such a matter."

[6] John Milton, "The Christian Doctrine" in *John Milton: Complete Poems and Major Prose*, ed. Merrit Y. Hughes (New York: The Odyssey Press, 1957).

out) the bare text of Scripture—read apart from sacred Tradition —appears to give us little reason to condemn polygamy and much encouragement in thinking it a good thing. Why do Evangelicals ignore Luther's and Milton's very logical arguments? Because, to the Evangelicals' great credit, in this case they've kept a Catholic approach to Scripture and do not rely on the Bible alone. They've kept an understanding of marriage derived from sacred Tradition which the Catholic Church preserved and which percolated down to Evangelicals through older Protestant traditions.

Marriage isn't the only area where Evangelicals benefit from their Catholic heritage. Despite a great deal of fuzziness in Scripture about the precise nature of pre-born human life, both Catholic and common Evangelical teaching unequivocally opposes abortion. Why? Because here again both Catholics and Evangelicals derive their teaching from apostolic Tradition, both written and unwritten. And, of course, Catholics and Evangelicals know what books belong in the New Testament not because the Bible tells them so, but because sacred Tradition does. In short, the reality isn't that Catholics rely on sacred Tradition and Evangelicals don't. The reality is that Catholics rely on sacred Tradition and know they do, while Evangelicals rely on sacred Tradition and usually don't know they do.[7]

On the Cutting Edge of Doctrinal Development

Just as a healthy newborn boy grows to become a man not a tree or a buffalo, apostolic Tradition is capable of real growth, but not mutation. That's why the Catholic Church staunchly insists she

---

[7] Rather than rewrite the full argument for the reality of sacred Tradition and the dependence of both Catholics and Protestants on it for the fullness of Christ's revelation, permit me to point readers with doubts and questions about sacred Tradition to my book *By What Authority: An Evangelical Discovers Catholic Tradition* (Huntington, Ind.: Our Sunday Visitor Books, 1996).

can admit no new public revelation and just as staunchly insists her Tradition develops. This way of talking about Tradition isn't bafflegab intended to justify compromises with paganism or the invention of unbiblical beliefs. Rather, as G. K. Chesterton says:

> The critics of Catholic theology seem to suppose that it is not so much an evolution as an evasion; that it is at best an adaptation. They fancy that its very success is the success of surrender. But that is not the natural meaning of the word Development. When we talk of a child being well-developed, we mean that he has grown bigger and stronger with his own strength; not that he is padded with borrowed pillows or walks on stilts to make him look taller. When we say that a puppy develops into a dog, we do not mean that his growth is a gradual compromise with a cat; we mean that he becomes more doggy and not less.[8]

The New Testament and post-apostolic periods in Church history offer a picture of the Dog of sacred Tradition flatly refusing any compromise with the Cat of Paganism—becoming "more doggy and not less." In that history we see an early Church one can only describe as "arch-conservative," clinging like a barnacle to what the apostles said and taught. That's why Polycarp, Ignatius and many others were martyred. That's why Irenaeus writes books like *Adversus Haereses*, repudiating all fashionable pagan upgrades on the faith of the apostles. For them, as for the present-day Catholic Church, Tradition is indeed complete. There will be no new improved versions à la Joseph Smith, no further revelations from some angel telling us that, on second thought, there is more than one God. For the Church has received all she needs in the written and unwritten Tradition that was complete with the death of the last apostle. The bishops' only job, as 1 and 2 Timothy and Titus command, is to guard that Tradition by preserving the message, whether written or unwritten, without addition or deletion. It is the very model of conservatism.

---

[8] G. K. Chesterton, *St. Thomas Aquinas: The Dumb Ox* (Garden City, N.Y.: Image Books, 1956), 27–28.

But it is a living conservatism—a living faith of the dead rather than a dead faith of the living. The fully formed "mustard plant" of the kingdom doesn't appear in the middle of the first century, the seventh, the sixteenth, or even today, at the beginning of the twenty-first. For new situations will always arise to demand that the Church make explicit some aspect of the Tradition that had hitherto been only implicit: encoded in the DNA of the mustard seed but not yet fully expressed in the branches and blossoms of the plant. How does the Church do this? By appealing, not to the Bible alone, but to the Bible in union with the apostolic Tradition of the Spirit-led body of Christ, governed by apostles and their successors who were given authority, in Paul's words, to "charge certain persons not to teach any different doctrine" (1 Tim. 1:3).

So it is that in our own day, for example, the Church condemns the evils of cloning human beings even though the bare text of Scripture has no words on the matter. But nobody in his five wits claims the present Church "invented" opposition to cloning from thin air. We all understand that the Church, by the very nature of her Tradition, has opposed such sinful manipulation of human beings for two thousand years. It merely took the folly of the modern push for cloning to cause the Church to apply Tradition to this concrete situation—and declare what she has always believed, even if she had never before had to say it about cloning.

To see this process at work, let us look at Acts 15 and the way that the very first development of sacred Tradition in the history of the Church took place. The genesis of this development was a controversy rife with theological, personal, and practical aspects: Did Gentile converts to the Christian faith need to be circumcised?

The Church, of course, began as a Jewish sect. Her members were Jews, her Lord was a Jew, and the only Scriptures she had when the argument over circumcision arose were Old Testament Scriptures. Not surprisingly then, Jewish Christians were thrown into a tailspin by the question of how Gentiles ought to be admitted to fellowship when confronted with a growing flood of such converts. It was particularly difficult because a significant portion of Gentile believers were none too eager to go under the knife. With the benefit of hindsight, we may think the issue was easy to resolve. But it wasn't. After all, Jesus had insisted that the Law —which required circumcision of all males who belonged to the covenant people—would not pass away and that following him required sacrifice and suffering. That was the problem confronting the Council of Jerusalem in Acts 15. How do we discern the will of God here?

Let us, for a moment, join the Council of Jerusalem in Acts 15 and imagine ourselves to be delegates from the mythical, Bible-only, hidden church of first century Evangelicals. How do we, as Bible-only Christians, respond to this problem?

Easy. We do a topical Bible study on circumcision! And when we do, what do we find? Well, we find that God gave Abraham the covenant of circumcision "as an everlasting covenant" (Gen. 17:7). It is the sign enjoined not only on descendants of Abraham, but upon "those who are not your offspring" (Gen. 17:12)—that is, on all men who want to join the covenant people by conversion (Ex. 12:48). So the Patriarchs are all circumcised. Moses is circumcised and the covenant of circumcision is renewed and reinforced in the Mosaic Law (Lev. 12:3). All the prophets are circumcised. And for good measure, as we look up from the Bible we are studying, we note that the apostles gathered around us are all circumcised and recall that even the Lord Jesus himself was circumcised (a fact a future companion of Paul's will eventually note, years from now, in Luke 2:21). And as the apostles around us are fond of recalling, Jesus used to say:

> Till heaven and earth pass away, not an iota, not a dot, will pass from the law until all is accomplished. Whoever then relaxes one of the least of these commandments and teaches men so, shall be called least in the kingdom of heaven; but he who does them and teaches them shall be called great in the kingdom of heaven (Matt. 5:18–19).

Meanwhile we also find Jesus silent about the idea that Gentiles are exempt from the immemorial requirement that men who want to join the covenant people undergo circumcision. Thus, on the basis of Scripture alone, the solution to the problem is obvious. Therefore, in Acts 15, the Church meets in council and, in light of all this plain scriptural teaching, declares . . .

. . . that circumcision for Gentile Christians is against the will of the God who does not change.

How do we Bible-only Evangelical delegates to the council respond? We could hold the first century Church to the same standard of Evangelical Bible-onlyism that we use when the modern Church says the same things about an unchanging gospel while proclaiming the dogmas of Mary's Immaculate Conception and Assumption. We could cry out in exasperation (as the Circumcision Party, in fact, did): "If this doctrine is the teaching of the God who does not change, then where the blazes is the circumcision exemption for Gentiles in Scripture and why did it not become a teaching of the Church until A.D. 48!? You are corrupting the word of God with the traditions of men to make the gospel more appealing to pagans!"

Or we could look at things a bit differently. We could decide to hold Marian doctrinal developments to the standards of the Council of Jerusalem. We can then propose that what happened at Jerusalem is the model for every single development of doctrine throughout Catholic history right down to the dogmatic definition of the Assumption of Mary in 1950.

Acts 15 in Slow-Motion Instant Replay

How does the interplay between the written and unwritten aspects of the gospel yield such apparently surprising results at the Council of Jerusalem? First of all, the men who met in Jerusalem didn't have a Bible—complete with New Testament—that could permit a topical study complete with Greek lexicons, learned commentaries, and all the tools of later biblical scholarship. Fortunately for us, the apostles had something far better than that. They had all had years of immersion into the common life, worship, and prayer of the Church, the very body of Christ to whom the Holy Spirit had been confided to explain all things (cf. John 16:13). Most of them had spent precious years actually living with Jesus, both before and after the Resurrection. They had actually heard his lips command them to preach the gospel to the whole world (cf. Matt. 28:19). And they had obeyed that command and personally witnessed astonishing results among the Gentiles. Peter had been visited by the Holy Spirit, who explained that Jesus willed the inclusion of the Gentiles into the Church—"What God has cleansed, you must not call common" (Acts 10:15)—and Peter had personally witnessed Cornelius and other Gentiles being granted the Holy Spirit without circumcision (cf. Acts 10:44–47). Paul and Barnabas had experienced the same thing among the Gentiles (cf. Acts 15:12), as had Philip among the Samaritans (cf. Acts 8:4).

These lived experiences crystallize as the apostles and elders gather, forming a kind of "apostolic lens" through which the Scriptural account of circumcision is read. That is why, when the Council meets, they do not do a topical Bible study on circumcision and derive their opinion on the matter from Scripture as the sole source of revelation. The first thing they do is start arguing with each other, illustrating the old Jewish proverb, "Two Jews, three opinions." When the arguing winds down, Peter stands up and appeals not to Scripture but to the apostolic Tradition of the Church and to his own Christ-delegated apostolic authority (cf. Luke 10:16). He says:

> Brethren, you know that in the early days God made choice among you, that by my mouth the Gentiles should hear the word of the gospel and believe. And God who knows the heart bore witness to them, giving them the Holy Spirit just as he did to us; and he made no distinction between us and them, but cleansed their hearts by faith. Now therefore why do you make trial of God by putting a yoke upon the neck of the disciples which neither our fathers nor

> we have been able to bear? But we believe that we shall be saved
> through the grace of the Lord Jesus, just as they will (Acts 15:7–11).

That last sentence is the key passage. That we are saved by the
grace of Jesus and not by keeping the ceremonial laws of Moses
is the central teaching of the Council of Jerusalem. It is an epoch-
making revelation since it will ultimately distinguish the Church
from rabbinic Judaism. Notice, however, that there's been no mention of Scripture at the council yet. Neither is there any appeal
to any pagan source. Rather, Peter's only appeal is to apostolic
authority and the Spirit's guidance of the Church.

After Peter speaks, Paul and Barnabas stand up and describe the
Spirit-led events which have marked their own missions: They
speak of miracles, signs and wonders among the uncircumcised
Gentiles. Like Peter, they also appeal, not to Scripture, but to
the faith given to the apostles by Jesus and to their own Christ-
delegated apostolic authority. It is only after this foundation has
been laid that the apostles finally get around to looking at Scripture, when James quotes the prophet Amos:

> After they finished speaking, James replied, "Brethren,
> listen to me. Symeon [Peter] has related how God first
> visited the Gentiles, to take out of them a people for his
> name. And with this the words of the prophets agree,
> as it is written,
>
> 'After this I will return,
> and I will rebuild the dwelling of David, which has
>   fallen;
> I will rebuild its ruins,
> and I will set it up,
> that the rest of men may seek the Lord,
> and all the Gentiles who are called by my name,
> says the Lord, who has made these things known from
>   of old'" (Acts 15:13–18).

Yet note this: neither James nor the Council derive from Amos
the idea that Gentiles don't have to be circumcised. Peter has

already settled that question before James cracks open the book of Amos, as James himself notes (cf. Acts 15:14). Rather, in light of the fullness of Christ's revelation through the lens of apostolic Tradition, James is able to see in the prophet Amos a witness to this ingathering of Gentiles and to the council's decision. Where have we seen this before?

We've seen it in the very process the Evangelists used to write the gospels. Just as Matthew didn't derive Jesus' virgin birth from Isaiah, so the Council at Jerusalem didn't derive the circumcision exemption from Amos. Rather, they're realizing the true scope and meaning of the gospel of Jesus Christ from their own apostolic experiences of Scripture and Tradition within the magisterial framework of the Church. James, Matthew, and everyone else at the council places the Church on the judge's seat and Scripture in the witness box, saying of the council's authoritative judgments that, "The words of the prophets *agree*" with them (Acts 15:15; emphasis added).

Thus, through the lens of apostolic Tradition, an Old Testament that seemed to say one thing about circumcision to the early Church is suddenly revealed to say something vastly different. Just as a whole bunch of colored dots on a page can be suddenly revealed, through the right perspective, to be a print of the Last Supper, so the bricks of Old Testament Scripture, which at first seemed to be building the Church into a synagogue of circumcision, are stacked by the trowel of the Church's magisterial authority and mortared with apostolic Tradition and turn out to make a cathedral of grace instead. The Council of Jerusalem, just like the Catholic Church, places Scripture in the context of the Church's Tradition and magisterial authority. The Council of Jerusalem, just like the Catholic Church, speaks with apostolic authority and declares, "It seemed good to the Holy Spirit and to *us* . . ." (Acts 15:29; emphasis added). And so, the Council of Jerusalem, just like the Catholic Church today, took a step under the guidance of the Spirit which, to Bible-only eyes, appears to flatly contradict Scripture—yet which, seen through the lens of sacred Tradition, upholds it (cf. Rom. 3:31). The council in union with Peter is guided by the Spirit to teach the truth that "we shall be saved through the grace of the Lord Jesus" and not by works of the Law, such as circumcision (Acts 15:11).

Two Scary Words

Every Church council in union with Peter has basically followed this biblical pattern ever since. Protected by the same Spirit who protected the Church in Acts 15, the Church has, at critical moments in its history, been guided by that Spirit to elaborate infallibly and clarify the implications of the revelation she has received. As result, she has periodically (albeit rarely) defined various dogmas of the faith which guide the flock in understanding the boundaries and depths of the apostolic teaching.

At the mention of those two scary words "infallibly" and "dogma," another set of questions arises. Ask the average person what infallible means and he will tell you it means "arrogant." Ask the average person what a dogma is and he will tell you it means "unthinking prejudice" or "close-minded opinion." So when we speak of the Church "infallibly promulgating dogmas" most modern folk think "That's when the Church says: 'Shut up,' and tells the faithful, 'If we want your opinion we'll give it to you.'"

This is not, however, what "infallibility" or "dogma" actually mean. To get the hang of what they do mean, let's shift gears from theology to science.

Science and theology have this in common: they're constrained to deal with facts, not fancy. But facts, of course, are tricky things. As any murder mystery fan knows, facts can point in all sorts of confusing directions and leave you puzzling for a very long time. It's the same with science and theology.

For a long time, there was open debate about the shape of the earth. Some thought it might be round since they noticed the way coastlines sank below the horizon when you sail away from them. By the third century B.C., the Greek astronomer and mathematician Eratosthenes had already estimated the earth's size by comparing shadows cast at two locations at noon and concluded that the earth must be a giant ball. But, of course, many other people trusted the obvious evidence of the senses: after all, in Kansas, at sea, or on the Russian steppe any idiot could see the world was flat. Just look at it!

Various schools of thought contended for years. Sometimes compromises were proposed, such as the Pizza Theory ("The world is round, yet flat!"). But eventually, a consensus in the educated community arose that Eratosthenes was right: The world was spherical. And so, among the educated it became, if you will, a "scientific dogma" that the earth was a sphere, centuries before it was possible to go into space and verify the dogma by direct observation. Science stopped debating the question of the earth's shape and those who continued to assert a flat earth were no longer taken seriously by anyone who knew what he was talking about.

So, a question: Does the dogma of a round earth stifle thought and crush the human quest for knowledge and truth? Nope. Instead, it does what all real dogma does: It says, "We've examined all the evidence soberly and come to the right conclusion. We're really done debating this question. Instead of ever learning and never coming to a knowledge of the truth (cf. 2 Tim 3:7), let's accept the fact that this matter is now settled and move on to talk about something more interesting." Indeed, the dogma of a spherical earth, like all real dogma, serves as the foundation upon which later explorers, wonderers, and questioners can stand as they conduct their next investigations of reality. Dogma is not the prohibition of thought. It is the conclusion of thought. It's what you get when you're done thinking something through.

People today who insist on rejecting the "dogma" of the spherical earth are not bold dissenters challenging the official lie. They are quacks and cranks who live on the fringes of real science and are, at best, a source of amusement. At their worst, they're a company of tiresome buffoons who complain about "oppression" and offer nutty theories about how the "truth" of the flat earth is being hidden from us by The Conspiracy. They have nothing important to say.

What's Infallibility?

So should we take our analogy even more literally and conclude that Catholic dogma, like a proven scientific idea, is simply the product of human wisdom? No, because theology and science part company as theology climbs on to an even higher plane of knowledge. For the Church enjoys a guarantee from God Incarnate that science does not: namely, that her solemn definitions of the faith will be protected from error by the guidance of the Spirit of Christ who leads us into all truth (cf. John 16:13) and who promises never to forsake the Church (Matt. 28:20). In short, Catholic dogma is infallible.

Now here's the surprising thing about infallibility: really arrogant people wouldn't stoop to claim it. For infallibility does not mean that the members of the Church (including the pope) are without sin or smarter than everybody else. On the contrary, it's a solemn teaching of the Church that everybody in the Church from pope to dogcatcher is a sinner. That's why the gift of infallibility is necessary. Infallibility is bestowed by God on the Church as a concession to our weakness, not as a reward for being especially clever, strong, or holy. If we want to understand it we have to imagine the magisterium of the Church, not as a James Bond who defeats every villain and escapes every trap by his own raw brilliance, but as a bumbling character in a farce who is miraculously guided through a dangerous and chaotic construction site, missing every swung beam and every dropped sack of cement along the way. Infallibility is the Church's confession of stupidity, blindness, and ineptitude—particularly among her leaders, who are tasked with preserving, articulating, and developing the teaching handed down to us. In short, the Church holds with gratitude to the promise which Christ gave her, that he would lead her (often by the nose) into all truth; not that she would figure truth out on her own by using her members' unsullied brilliance and virtue.

That is why infallibility doesn't mean never having to say you're sorry. Catholics say they're sorry in every penitential rite of every Mass. The Church is not infallible because Catholics are perfect, but because nobody in the earthly Church is perfect, so the Holy Spirit has to constantly act to ensure we dumb humans don't fumble the gospel. God holds the Church's hand every step of the way and makes sure she doesn't spill the wine of revelation, because Catholics are such sin-plagued and error-prone klutzes that, without the Holy Spirit, we'd have lost track of the gospel half an hour after Pentecost. That's all infallibility means. And you can see it at work, not just in the circumcision controversy of Acts 15, but in the raging controversy confronted by the Church several hundred years later, when people began wondering again about Jesus' question: "Who do you say that I am?" (Matt. 16:15).

The Discovery of the Trinity

The quest to clearly answer that question forced Christians to hold onto two basic tenets of Christian teaching:

1. That God revealed himself in a progressive revelation that begins with Genesis and was not completed till the death of the last apostle,[9] and;

2. Since then, the Church's understanding of God's revelation has deepened and developed.

Because of these immovable facts, it's not inaccurate to say that the truth about Jesus' identity was not invented but discovered by the Church. For the Church, so far from creating anything, simply followed the clues left by God in his complete revelation given through Scripture and Tradition.

The clues were essentially as follows:

---

[9] Please note that the belief that revelation closed with the death of the last apostle is held by both Catholics and Evangelicals and yet is another point of sacred Tradition that is not explicitly attested by Scripture.

CLUE 1: There is but one God. This is the theme drummed into Israel by the tradition and Scripture of both the Law and the prophets. "Hear O Israel: The LORD our God is one LORD!" (Deut. 6:4) is the very heart and soul of the Old Testament. Alone among all the ancient nations of the earth, Israel is chosen by God to be the one people in covenant with this one God. Alone among the nations of the earth, Israel is held to fidelity to this one God through sin, disaster, enslavement, deportation, conquest and political humiliation. That there is one God is the unshakable revelation given to the Jews.

CLUE 2: God will send the Messiah. This too is drummed into Israel's consciousness over and over again by the prophets. The complete portrait of this Messiah isn't clear at first: Healer, Bringer of Peace, Conquering Davidic King, Suffering Servant, all these hints and more roil about in the mix—until Jesus unites them all in his person.

CLUE 3: The Messiah is God. While Jesus emphasizes the ancient truth that God is one and there are no other gods, he also forgives sins, which (rightly) prompts the Pharisees and Jesus' own disciples to ask "Who can forgive sins but God alone?" (Mark 2:7). Jesus calls himself the Son of David, but also implies that he is "David's Lord" (cf. Mark 12:35–37). He applies the name "I AM" to himself—the very name of God revealed to Moses (cf. Ex. 3:14; John 8:58). In short, Jesus claims to be the Messiah and the one God who led Israel through the wilderness, gave the Law, and called the prophets.

CLUE 4: The Messiah and God the Father are "one" yet are different persons, as is the Holy Spirit. Jesus is, by his own account, somehow distinct from the one he calls "my Father" (John 8:38), who is "greater than I" (John 14:28). But at the same time, Jesus insists "I and the Father are one" (John 10:30). Moreover, Jesus teaches there is yet another—a counselor, comforter and Spirit of Truth—who proceeds from the Father and the Son (John 14:16–17; 15:26; Gal. 4:6). And Jesus commands that his disciples baptize all nations in the name of the Father, Son, and Holy Spirit (Matt. 28:19).

These "clues" outline the basic problem set by the Christian revelation. The faith of the Church is identical to Israel's in one respect: There is but one God. But the Church also sees further revelation, summed up in Simon Peter's declaration: "You are the Christ, the Son of the living God" (Matt. 16:16). And all this is further complicated by the fact that Jesus and his apostles teach that the Spirit (or Holy Spirit or Spirit of Jesus or Spirit of Truth or Advocate as he is variously called in the New Testament) is also a personal being who convinces the world of sin, gives graces, enlightens, and guides the Church into all truth.

How then does the Church piece together these mysterious revelations? Very slowly, and with a conscious reliance on the Spirit of Truth to, in fact, do what Christ promised and guide the Church into all truth (cf. John 16:13).

Various attempts to reconcile the clues are proposed by various early theologians. Some have certain insights into the Truth (for example, it's a second century Christian, Tertullian, who coins the term "Trinity"). Yet early Christians also struggle with their inability to understand the gospel—nearly always a result of the fact that these early Christian thinkers try to make certain clues "fit" by suppressing or ignoring other clues. For instance, some guarded the truth that God is one by denying that the three Persons are distinct. They said God was the Father before the Incarnation, the Son during the Incarnation, and the Spirit since the Ascension —entirely ignoring the fact that Jesus prayed to the Father; that the Father spoke to Jesus; that Jesus asked for the Holy Spirit to be sent and the Father sent the Holy Spirit; and that the Church prays and baptizes in the name of all three. Others emphasized the distinctness of the persons and wound up advocating the polytheistic worship of three Gods. Still others, like Marcion, floated a theory that the Old Testament God is bad while Jesus is the good God of the New Testament, here to rescue us from the bad one.

All these theories (and many others) were weighed and sifted in the Church for nearly three hundred years, while the Church continually issued definitions of what she did not believe till finally a theory appeared which seemed (like the devil imitating Christ) to explain all the biblical data and yet which struck at the very heart of the Church's Faith: Arianism.

Arius was a fourth century theologian who hit upon the novel notion that Jesus was not God, but a supernatural created being. He was, said Arius, vastly superior to us (as an archangel is) but he was still created and not of one being with the Father. Arius argued that various Scriptures—such as "I and the Father are one" (John 10:30)—referred to the oneness of Jesus' will with the Father's, not the oneness of his being. And since Jesus was a creature, according to Arius, worshipping him as God was, in fact, a sin. But since Jesus is so vastly superior to all other creatures, we could speak of him as a "god" compared to us, but not identify him with the "Big G" God who is Creator of all. This 'simple'' theory, while appearing to be a faithful rendering of Scripture, completely denies the ancient faith that Jesus is literally "God with us." If Arius was right, then Jesus' death, like the death of any other creature, could neither save from sin nor bestow on us what the apostles had promised: a participation in the divine nature (cf. 2 Pet. 1:4). For even Jesus cannot give what he does not have, and if he does not have divine life, he cannot give it to us.

How did the Church respond? She did what the apostles did and assembled the bishops in council, first at Nicaea and, later, at Constantinople. At these councils the Church reasserted the traditional teaching that God was indeed one (as Arius had insisted), as well as the traditional teaching that Jesus' oneness with the Father and the Spirit is a oneness of three Persons who are one God. The councils reaffirmed not only that the Word was with God (as Arius taught) but that the Word was God (as John 1:1 taught). In so doing, the Church took a historic step away from her earlier policy of saying what should not be believed about the Godhead, and affirmed what must be believed. The Church chose a series of careful descriptions ("God from God, Light from Light, True God from True God, begotten, not made, one in being with the Father") summarizing what she asserted about Jesus against all the various attempts to suppress portions of the biblical data in favor of false "simplicity."

So nothing was invented by the Church with respect to the Trinity. The Church did not suddenly decide to make Jesus the "Son of God" at Nicaea. She merely clarified with extraordinary precision what was meant by that centuries-old confession that Jesus is the Son of God. The Church sought to prevent a "simplifying" invention by Arius and to remain true to all the biblical data, not just those pieces of it Arius liked. Paradoxically, in fighting that invention, the Church discovered a far deeper understanding of what she had always believed and formulated it in the Nicene Creed.

Three Things to Note

First, Dan Brown is once again shown to be full of hooey. For his claim that "until [Nicaea], Jesus was viewed by his followers as a mortal prophet" is now shown to be completely worthless. The truth is, not only was Nicaea simply restating what the Church had always taught about Jesus in opposition to a fresh assault by Arius, but Arius himself, as much as his orthodox opponents, would have laughed to scorn Dan Brown's suggestion that Jesus was just a mortal prophet. For Arius, Jesus was not some guy from Nazareth with a girlfriend and a New Age longing for the Sacred Feminine. He was an immensely powerful supernatural being second only to God himself. Compared to Brown, Arius is practically a Catholic.

Second, it must be noted that what Nicaea was doing, in the final analysis, was not making up new revelation, but unpacking the full implication of old revelation: namely, Peter's declaration "You are the Christ, the Son of the living God" (Matt. 16:16). Nicaea was engaged in one monumental exploration of the universe of wonder enfolded into those ten words. The lesson of Nicaea is that the meaning of life, the universe and everything is compressed into Peter's words as the mustard plant is compressed into the seed and it's the task of the Church to unpack that meaning.

That's why Christian theology has to be complicated. Theology is the study of supernatural life just as biology is the study of natural life. We make no more sense demanding that theology —the Queen of the Sciences—make itself simple for our benefit than we would in demanding that biology simplify itself by declaring that cells are filled with a featureless jelly and not all those chromosomes, ribosomes, mitochondria, and the rest. It is, says Proverbs 25:2, the "glory of kings" to search out matters belonging to God. As Christians, we should accept nothing less.

All this brings us to our third point: according to the Church, every one of the Catholic Church's doctrinal developments—all the way down to the Assumption of Mary—proceeds in exactly the same fashion as the development of doctrine at the Council of Nicaea. Each Marian teaching—like each Christological teaching —is rooted in written and unwritten apostolic Tradition —not paganism—and draws all its life from there. Likewise, each Marian teaching is reflected in the text of Scripture either implicitly or explicitly, but the connection of the text to the doctrine cannot always be seen clearly apart from the Tradition as it's discerned by the body of Christ.

Realizing this, I realized I had to break an old habit that, despite my newfound awareness of sacred Tradition, had continued up till then to affect the way I thought about Catholic Marian teaching. It was the habit of looking for a biblical basis for this and that Catholic teaching. For the simple fact was that the authors of the New Testament did not base their faith on the Bible. They based it on apostolic Tradition, both written and unwritten, which is incarnate in the Church. For them, this Tradition is a unified whole, like a weave. And it maintains its integrity even as it grows from mustard seed to mustard plant. Because of that, the question that always faced the Church was not "Is this Bible-based?," but "Is this apostolic?"

Second, and more subtly, everything we have looked at so far—from Evangelical jitters about Mary, to the attempted debunking of the Virgin Birth, to Luke's account of the Nativity, to John's vision of the woman as the mother of the One who rules the nations with a rod of iron—demonstrates in various ways something Catholic theology is constantly saying and Evangelicals constantly fail to hear: namely, that the whole point about Mary is that the point is not about Mary.

6

A Referred Life

No you, no me.
No water, then there's no sea.
Without your love I cease to be.
No you, no me.

—Bob Halligan, Jr.

Consider: Just as the ark of the covenant would be nothing but a gold box if it weren't for the God of Israel who made it holy, so Mary would be of absolutely no consequence to us if not for her Son. It is because the woman is the mother of the "male child" that she matters at all. If he had not been born, you never would have heard of her. Curiously, every time you look at her, you find you are actually looking at someone or something else. After all, the question "Where is the Assumption of Mary in the Bible?" is not really about Mary. It's a question about the validity of Christ's sacred Tradition and the authority of Christ's Church. "Why should I pray to Mary?" is not a question about Mary. It's a question about the relationship of the living and the dead in Christ. "Do Catholics worship Mary?" is not a question about Mary. It's a question about whether Catholics really worship Christ. In short, Evangelical jitters about Mary both pay homage to and yet overlook the central truth about Mary that the Catholic Church wants us to see: that Mary's life, in its entirety, is a referred life.

No Mary, No Salvation

John, with characteristic economy of expression, captures this referred life in Mary's own words: "Do whatever he tells you"

(John 2:5). Luke does it in another way by recording her words, "Behold, I am the handmaid of the Lord; let it be to me according to your word" (Luke 1:38). If this were all the Church had to say about her, Evangelicals would be more than happy to let the matter rest there. What baffles so many non-Catholics is the Church's tendency to keep referring us to her. "*Ad Iesum per Mariam!*" say Catholics, "To Jesus through Mary!" Hearing this, many non-Catholics nervously respond, "Isn't Christianity supposed be about a relationship with Jesus Christ? Why do Catholics focus on Mary so much? Doesn't salvation come to us through him and not her?"

If, by those questions we mean to ask, "Wasn't it, after all, Jesus who died upon the cross and rose from the dead, who ascended into Heaven and whose Spirit is now poured out on those who believe in him?", then the obvious answer is "yes." But when I reflected on the matter as an Evangelical, I came to realize that salvation was nonetheless inextricably bound up with Mary, precisely because she's totally referred to Christ. For the hands and feet through which the nails were pounded, and the blood that was poured out for our salvation were given to Jesus Christ by Mary through her freely chosen "Yes" to God. Without Mary, there was no human nature for the Second Person of the Trinity to assume. Without that human nature, there could have been no death on the cross, since God cannot, in his deity, die. Without his death on the cross, there could be no Resurrection. Without his Resurrection, there could be no salvation.

So the simple fact is: no Mary, no salvation.

Mary's Life Is Like Our Own

In the Evangelical world, such an observation typically provokes a flurry of highly speculative claims that "God would have just chosen somebody else if Mary had said no." But by the time I had begun to realize all these things about Mary, I had been immunized against such "alternative history" speculations by C. S.

Lewis' Aslan, who said with great common sense, "no one is ever told what would have happened."[1] In plain fact, we don't know what God might have done. We only know what he did. Therefore, whatever we make of "To Jesus through Mary" it's at least perfectly plain that, in this universe, Jesus comes to the world through her. So it is, I realized, quite biblical to speak as Irenaeus did long ago and note that she "being obedient, was made the cause of salvation for herself and for the whole human race."[2]

Thinking about Mary's referred life also started me thinking about how many other people in my life Jesus came through to get to me. He came to me, for instance, through my Evangelical friend Sandy, who brought me Pepto-Bismol when I was desperately sick with flu in college, thereby making this unbeliever first notice the love of Jesus working through one of his saints. He came to me through the Evangelical believers on my dorm floor: the first Christians to speak the word of God to me. He came to me through the love of my parents and family. He came to me through various Christian teachers on the radio and TV. He came to me through the work of C. S. Lewis, G. K. Chesterton, Peter Kreeft, and Dorothy L. Sayers, and through various friends too numerous to count who prayed for me, helped me, supported me and buoyed me through the challenges of life. He came to me through my wife, through Scripture, through moments of perfect beauty and through times of terrible trial. In fact, the more I looked at it, the more it seemed to me that God virtually always comes to us through some creature. And when he does that, some glow of his glory is left on the creature, like the radiance on Moses' face (cf. Ex. 34:29–35). But at the same time it remains clear the glory is God's, not something the creature could claim for himself.

In other words, what Mary is in full by her total "Yes" to God, so all creatures—and especially all saints—are in some degree as

---

[1] C. S. Lewis, *The Voyage of the Dawn Treader* (New York: Collier, 1970), 136.

[2] Irenaeus, *Adversus Haereses*, 3, 22, 4.

well by the grace of God. For we all live lives that are referred—
and referred, not just to God, but to other creatures. A father's
and a husband's life is referred to his family, which is why Paul
tells husbands to "love your wives, as Christ loved the church
and gave himself up for her" (Eph. 5:25) and bids them to bring
up children "in the discipline and instruction of the Lord" (Eph.
6:4). Likewise, the lives of wives and mothers are referred to their
husbands and their children. The life of a citizen is, to a certain
degree, referred to the life of the community, while the life of a
ruler is referred to the good of the citizen. Of course, there are
limits to all this. A ruler, for example, is referred to his community, but not to the degree that he may deliberately kill innocent
life "for the good of the Fatherland." But within the parameters
of God's plan, Christian life must be lived in the awareness that
we're members not merely of Christ alone, but of Christ among his
people—that we're members of "one another" as well (cf. Rom.
12:5).

Disciples Model Discipleship

Because of this, Scripture does not simply point us to Jesus Christ
and say "Imitate him and nobody else." Rather, the inspired writers say, "Be imitators of me, as I am of Christ" (1 Cor. 11:1) and
call us likewise to see Jesus through the lives of others who are
joined to Christ. For there is one thing even Jesus Christ cannot
do: he cannot show us what it looks like to be a disciple of Jesus
Christ. Only a disciple of Jesus Christ can do that. That's why we
have a sort of impromptu roll call of the saints in Hebrews 11.
We are not merely to look to Christ directly; we are also to look
to those models because in them, we see Christ reflected in a new
and deeper way. That's why Paul prays "that the God of our Lord
Jesus Christ, the Father of glory, may give you a spirit of wisdom
and of revelation in the knowledge of him, having the eyes of your
hearts enlightened, that you may know what is the hope to which
he has called you, what are the riches of his glorious inheritance
in the saints" (Eph. 1:17–18; emphasis added).

Paul's notion that we meet Jesus not merely directly, but through his saints as well, is one he comes by honestly. For when Jesus revealed himself to a Pharisee bent on persecuting followers of the Way, he did not say, "Saul, Saul, why do you persecute my followers?" Rather, the Lord taught him to see the Church referred to himself with the words "Saul, Saul, why do you persecute *me*?" (Acts 9:4; emphasis added). The head and the body are one, says Jesus. And because of this, the story of Saul's conversion does not end on the Damascus road. For the next thing Jesus does is refer Saul back to "the church, which is his body, the fulness of him who fills all in all" (Eph. 1:22–23). And so, the Church comes to him in the person of Ananias, who baptizes him (cf. Acts 9:10–19), whereupon Saul makes a stab at preaching the gospel in Damascus. In short, Baptism leads to action, and action to fruitfulness—and persecution (cf. Acts 9:20–25). This, after a period of contemplation, eventually leads Saul once again to the Church (cf. Gal. 1:17–18; Acts 9:26–30), which (after about a decade of training in the faith) leads again to action (cf. Acts 13:1–3) and, from action to fruitfulness—and persecution (see the rest of the life of Paul).

The Trinitarian Dance of Salvation

If this pattern is starting to look vaguely familiar, it's because, as we have already seen, it's the pattern of self-sacrifice, death, and resurrection in Jesus Christ. It's the pattern summed up by our Lord when he said:

> Truly, truly, I say to you, unless a grain of wheat falls into the earth and dies, it remains alone; but if it dies, it bears much fruit. He who loves his life loses it, and he who hates his life in this world will keep it for eternal life. If any one serves me, he must follow me; and where I am, there shall my servant be also; if any one serves me, the Father will honor him (John 12:24–26).

It's the pattern that is played out when Jesus takes the bread, gives thanks, breaks it, and gives it to his disciples, just as the disciples themselves are offered with thanks to the Father, their lives too are broken in service and even martyrdom, and the blood of the martyrs becomes "the seed of the Church."[3]

That mystical pattern of exchange is at the heart of reality because it is at the heart of God. It is how the life of God proceeds and it is precisely this pattern of exchange Jesus speaks of when he prays:

> that they may all be one; even as thou, Father, art in me, and I in thee, that they also may be in us, so that the world may believe that thou hast sent me. The glory which thou hast given me I have given to them, that they may be one even as we are one, I in them and thou in me, that they may become perfectly one, so that the world may know that thou hast sent me and hast loved them even as thou hast loved me (John 17:21–23).

It was the attempt to reject this mystical pattern of exchange of self for the other in the love of the Trinity that not only made the devil the devil, but introduced sin into the world. As C. S. Lewis writes:

> The golden apple of selfhood, thrown among the false gods, became an apple of discord because they scrambled for it. They did not know the first rule of the holy game, which is that every player must by all means touch the ball and then immediately pass it on. To be found with it in your hands is a fault; to cling to it, death. But when it flies to and fro among the players too swift for eye to follow, and the great master Himself leads the revelry, giving Himself eternally to His creatures in the generation, and back to Himself in the sacrifice, of the Word, then indeed the eternal dance "makes Heaven drowsy with the harmony."[4]

In short, the fully Christian life is not just "me and Jesus." It is not even just "me and the Father, Son, and Holy Spirit." It is the Father giving his life to the Son, and his Son giving himself back to the Father, and the Holy Spirit proceeding like a gorgeous

---

[3] Tertullian, *Apologeticum*, 50, 13.

[4] C. S. Lewis, *The Problem of Pain* (New York: Macmillan, 1976), 153.

musical chord from the love of the Father and the Son to fill the life of the Church. For in this eternal act of love, we are swept up and made "partakers of the divine nature" (2 Pet. 1:4) by Baptism into the Father, Son and Holy Spirit, so that the Church—the lives of all those who are part of Christ's self-offering to the Father —becomes part of the gift we receive from the Father and give back to him through the Son. The ancient Church even coined a word to describe this reality—*perichoresis*—that, like Lewis, borrows from the vocabulary of dance (*peri* = around and *choreuo* = dance) to try to portray the way in which God himself is a community of love among the Three Persons and how salvation is, so to speak, the process of learning the steps of that dance among all the saints of the Church as they're led by the Master.

God Has Loves, Not Reasons

This bears directly on the question of why the Church refers us not just to Jesus, but to Mary and the other saints. For at the heart of the Christian life is the fundamental belief that God is love and that the world was not created out of grim economic necessity with only enough life and love available to give to God and none left over for his creatures. Rather, Scripture teaches that we are made out of God's abundant and overflowing life, which he desires to share with his creatures.

My own Evangelical tradition had tended to lead me away from this insight by training me to think in rigidly economical terms about the glory of God. We asked why Mary or the saints are "necessary" to Catholic piety. We wanted to know what the "use" was of speaking of their glory or asking for their prayers. We asked why paying attention to Mary and other saints didn't "deprive" God of glory and upset the "economy of salvation."

But in the middle of all this I was struck by a startling biblical truth explained in a wonderful book called *The Supper of the Lamb* by Robert Farrar Capon. Capon explained that to approach anything in creation with the question "Why is this necessary?"

or "What's the use of this?" is to be fundamentally tone deaf to God. Asking whether flowers, galaxies, beautiful weather, or the Virgin Mary are "necessary" or "useful" makes no sense, says Capon, because none of creation is necessary or useful to its Creator. The whole universe exists because God just thought it was a good idea and gratuitously loved it into being. "God," says Capon, "has loves, not reasons."[5]

This leads to some startling realizations. For example, it leads to the realization that life is about play at least much as it's about work. It leads to the subversive possibility that God is not a human resources manager fretting about economic theory, parsimonious allocation of limited glory resources and the need to eliminate an oversized workforce of saints who are making his job unnecessary. It leads to the possibility that eternal confusion awaits all those with the notion that the glory of God is a zero-sum game. As Capon points out, there is in the very idea of creation something extravagant, artistic, and playful. God, after all, didn't have to create anything. He was under no economic necessity and he has never been constrained by worries about resource distribution and time management. If he (who needs nothing, after all) "needed" more resources, he could just make them *ex nihilo*. He's got all the time in eternity. Creation, says Capon, is "radically unnecessary."[6]

This means that if God does not create out of need or utility, there is only one other explanation: He creates for love. He creates just because he wants to. He creates as an artist creates, not as a harried foreman with a quota on a production line creates. He creates because creation is a lovely and delicious thing, not because creation is a necessary thing. And we, who are made in his image, are therefore missing the entire point of the whole extravagant show if we focus exclusively on economics and never get it into our hearts that these human economic systems are no

---

[5] Robert Farrar Capon, *The Supper of the Lamb: A Culinary Reflection* (Garden City, N.Y.: Doubleday, 1978), 86.

[6] *Ibid.*, 85.

more the central story of existence than the cost of paint is the central story of the Sistine Chapel.

This is why the economic approach can be so right about small things and yet so disastrously wrong about big things. It is true that economics plays a role in human existence. It is not true that it plays the biggest role. As Chesterton observes:

> Cows may be purely economic, in the sense that we cannot see that they do much beyond grazing and seeking better grazing-grounds; and that is why a history of cows in twelve volumes would not be very lively reading. Sheep and goats may be pure economists in their external action at least; but that is why the sheep has hardly been a hero of epic wars and empires thought worthy of detailed narration; and even the more active quadruped has not inspired a book for boys called Golden Deeds of Gallant Goats or any similar title. But so far from the movements that make up the story of man being economic, we may say that the story only begins where the motive of the cows and sheep leaves off.[7]

In short, human beings, at their most human, do things that make no sense to economists—because they're like God. They fall in love. They take vows of poverty, chastity, and obedience. They write sonnets, paint cave walls, invent break dancing and perform thought experiments about relativity during their lunch hours working at the patent office. They go frittering away a perfectly useful day of productive work just to romp in the sun, eat heartily, and thank God that grass is green, wind is sweet, the universe is a strange place, and life is a gift.

It is the fact that "the world will always be more delicious than it is useful"[8] that was so breathtaking to me. For it meant, says Capon, that not just Mary, but everything was radically unnecessary. Creation is "the orange peel hung on God's chandelier, the wishbone in his kitchen closet. He likes it; therefore it stays."[9]

---

[7] G. K. Chesterton, *The Everlasting Man* (San Francisco: Ignatius Press, 1993), 137.

[8] Capon, *The Supper of the Lamb*, 40.

[9] *Ibid.*, 5.

God was not under some fatal obligation to make or choose Mary, just as he was not under any obligation to make or redeem us. He just did so out of bounty, freely and with delight, as a painter chooses his brush, oils, and canvas. In Mary, the whole of God's delight in us could be seen at its most playful and at its most solemn, involving us in his life and work, not because he needed us, but because he rejoiced to have it so. In short, God chose Mary as he chose us: not because he needed her, but because he loved her freely. And since "where the Spirit of the Lord is, there is freedom" (2 Cor. 3:17) her "yes" to him was free—and real—too. So she was deserving of honor (and imitation) just as we honor and imitate the self-sacrificial love of both the soldiers who laid down everything for the love of country and the mothers who bravely supported them as they went to their deaths. For both Jesus and the mother who courageously let the sword pierce her heart (cf. Luke 2:34–35; John 19:34) are worthy of such honor.

That train of thought gave me pause. But even that thought, powerful though it was, didn't move me to cry out "*Ad Iesum per Mariam!*" Old mental tapes are hard to erase. And the thought of "going to Jesus through Mary" still seemed to me, as it does to most Evangelicals, like a needless complication of the gospel. It still sounded as though Catholics thought of Mary as a kind of secretary for a busy executive ("May I ask who is calling? I'm sorry, sir, but you need to make an appointment with me before you can talk to Jesus. He's a very busy man. Besides, you'll find that I'm much nicer than he is.")

My head might have been growing more Catholic, but my gut was still deeply Evangelical: something in me still complained, "Okay. I can see the whole 'Mary is referred to Jesus' thing. But why Marian dogmas? Even if we grant that Mary is really important to a lot of Catholics, why not let those who want to do so believe what they like and leave the rest of us alone? Why should a Protestant, entering the Church, be bound to believe in, say, the Assumption of Mary on pain of being told by the pope 'if anyone, which God forbid, should dare willfully to deny or to call into doubt that which we have defined, let him know that he has fallen away completely from the divine and Catholic Faith.' "[10]

Attacking Jesus Through Mary

I might still be standing there puzzling over this if something odd hadn't happened: I began to realize that whether or not we Evangelicals got to Jesus through Mary, his enemies most certainly did.

For what, after all, was the attack on the Virgin Birth we discussed above? Certainly it wasn't an attack on Mary; it was an attack on Christ himself and on the integrity of his gospel. And, of course, the Church's defense of the Virgin Birth isn't about Mary either. It's about defending the faith from attacks on Christ and on the integrity of his gospel.

That put things in a new light and it helped me see for the first time why the Church does and does not define certain things as dogma. What I mean is this: Have you ever noticed that the Church has never dogmatically proclaimed that Mary had red blood? Nothing could be a more biblical truth. She was a Jew of the house of David, a daughter of Abraham, and a member of the species *homo sapiens*. Yet even though "Mary has red blood" is one of the incontestable facts of Scripture and something verifiable by both apostolic Tradition and even scientific observation, the Catholic Church has never dogmatically defined that Mary's blood was red. Why not?

Because though it's a truth about Mary, it's a truth that doesn't matter. Nobody denies it. Nobody argues against it. And if somebody did, everybody else would politely turn away and talk about something normal people talk about. For similar reasons, the Church has never promulgated a dogma that Jesus often drank water, or that Mary ate bread, or that both of them breathed

---

[10] Pope Pius XII, *Munificentissimus Deus*, 45.

oxygen. Such propositions have never been controversial, so they've never been something the Church had to protect with the shield of dogma.

If the Virgin Birth were the only issue involving Mary that had ever been attacked in the long history of assaults on the gospel of Jesus Christ, then it might well be possible there would be no other Marian doctrines. But the fact is, throughout the history of the Church, enemies of Christ have attacked him, not directly, but as Satan did in the Garden of Eden: through those he loves. *The Da Vinci Code* is but the latest example of that ancient pattern. Very rarely does a critic of Christianity go after Jesus himself. In the vast majority of cases, the attack on Jesus proceeds as an attack on the body of Christ that, as the tired refrain goes, supplanted the "Jesus of history" with the "Christ of faith." That's what links together the mutually contradictory assertions from various foes of Christianity who, instead of claiming (like Marcion) that the body of Christ has corrupted the truth and made Jesus into a Jew or claiming (like Dan Brown) that the body of Christ has corrupted the truth and made him into God, instead tell us that the body of Christ has corrupted the truth(s) that

- Jesus was a woman.[11]

- Jesus was a space alien and is buried in Japan.[12]

- Jesus survived the crucifixion and is buried in Kashmir.[13]

- Jesus was a Buddhist.[14]

---

[11] *Judith Christ of Nazareth: The Gospels of the Bible, Corrected to Reflect That Christ Was a Woman, Extracted from the Books of Matthew, Mark, Luke, and John* (Washington, D.C.: LBI Law and Business Institute, 2003).

[12] Available at http://www.thiaoouba.com/tomb.htm as of September 29, 2008.

[13] Available at http://en.wikipedia.org/wiki/Yuz_Asaf as of September 29, 2008.

[14] Available at http://www.google.com/Top/Society/Religion_and_Spiritual ity/Buddhism/Buddhism_and_Other_Religions/Christianity/Jesus-Was-a-Bud dhist_Theories/ as of September 29, 2008.

- Jesus was a Muslim.[15]

- Jesus was a Mormon.[16]

- Jesus was a magician.[17]

- Jesus was a Gnostic.[18]

- Jesus was the son of Mary and a Roman soldier.[19]

- Jesus never existed.[20]

- Jesus was never executed.[21]

- Jesus was a social revolutionary[22] when he was not a mere Mediterranean peasant.[23]

- Jesus was an itinerant visionary whose real teachings exist only in distorted, fragmented form.[24]

- Jesus was insane.[25] [26]

---

[15] Available at http://www.jesusthemuslim.com/ as of September 29, 2008.

[16] Available at http://www.aboutjesuschrist.org/ as of September 29, 2008.

[17] Available at http://www.colorado.edu/philosophy/vstenger/RelSci/Magi cian.html as of September 29, 2008.

[18] Available at http://altreligion.about.com/od/gnosticjesus/Gnostic_Jesus .htm as of September 29, 2008.

[19] Available at http://judaism.about.com/od/beliefs/a/jesus.htm as of September 29, 2008.

[20] Available at http://www.jesusneverexisted.com as of September 29, 2008.

[21] http://www.geocities.com/athens/delphi/1340/jesus_in_india.htm

[22] John Dominic Crossan, *Jesus: A Revolutionary Biography* (New York: HarperOne, 1995).

[23] John Dominic Crossan, *The Historical Jesus: The Life of a Mediterranean Jewish Peasant* (New York: HarperOne, 1993).

[24] Robert Walter Funk, *Honest to Jesus: Jesus for a New Millennium* (San Francisco: Harper San Francisco, 1996).

[25] See http://www.religionislies.com/deranged.html.

[26] For this list, I am indebted to Anthony Sacramone, "Robo-Jesus," *First Things'* On the Square blog, January 27, 2007. Available at http://firstthings .com/onthesquare/?p=577 as of September 29, 2008.

The key to every single one of these claims is that they attack Jesus by attacking the Church. As ever, "the accuser of the brethren . . . accuses them day and night before our God" (Rev. 12:10). And so, the Church has found it necessary to fight, not only to defend the truth of Jesus, but also those who "keep the commandments of God and bear testimony to Jesus" (Rev. 12:17).

This doesn't mean that any criticism of the Church or of Christians is really just a Satanic attack on Christ. To be sure, there are bad Christians who disgrace the gospel. There always have been such Christians, ever since Judas. But even so, the reality is that Jesus promised the Church he will remain with her always, guide her into all truth by his Spirit, and thereby ensure that the gates of Hell shall not prevail against her (cf. Matt. 28:20; John 16:13; Matt. 16:18). Therefore, because Mary is a figure of holy Church as Revelation 12 and the Fathers of the Church make clear, it follows that when attacks on Jesus are made via his body, those attacks necessarily involve Mary. And that—as we shall see in Volume Two: *A Woman Protects a Man*—is the point, not only of the dogma of the Virgin Birth, but of all the Church's dogmas about Mary.

Bibliography

Michael J. Aquilina, *The Fathers of the Early Church: An Introduction to the First Christian Fathers* (Huntington, Ind.: Our Sunday Visitor, 1999).

Georges Bernanos, *The Diary of a Country Priest* (Chicago: Thomas More Press, 1983).

Robert Farrar Capon, *The Supper of the Lamb: A Culinary Reflection* (Garden City, N.Y.: Doubleday, 1978).

G. K. Chesterton, *The Everlasting Man* (San Francisco: Ignatius Press, 1995). Also available at http://wikilivres.info/w/index.php/The_Everlasting_Man.

———. *Orthodoxy* (San Francisco: Ignatius Press, 1995). Also available at http://ccel.org/ccel/chesterton/orthodoxy.titlepage.html.

———. *St. Thomas Aquinas: The Dumb Ox* (Garden City, N.Y.: Image, 1974). Also available at http://wikilivres.info/w/index.php/St._Thomas_Aquinas:_The_Dumb_Ox.

Donald DeMarco and Benjamin Wiker, *Architects of the Culture of Death* (San Francisco: Ignatius Press, 2004).

Michael Dubruiel and Amy Welborn, *Praying the Rosary: With the Joyful, Luminous, Sorrowful, and Glorious Mysteries* (Huntington, Ind.: Our Sunday Visitor, 2005).

Austin Marsden Farrer, *A Rebirth of Images: The Making of St. John's Apocalypse* (Albany: State University of New York Press, 1986).

Daniel J. Flynn, *Intellectual Morons: How Ideology Makes Smart People Fall for Stupid Ideas* (New York: Crown Forum, 2004).

Fr. Benedict Groeschel, *The Rosary: Chain of Hope* (San Francisco: Ignatius Press, 2003).

————. *A Still, Small Voice: A Practical Guide on Reported Revelations* (San Francisco: Ignatius Press, 1993).

Scott Hahn, *Hail, Holy Queen: The Mother of God in the Word of God* (New York: Doubleday, 2001).

————. *The Lamb's Supper: The Mass As Heaven on Earth* (New York: Doubleday, 1999).

John Hardon, S.J., *The Catholic Catechism* (Garden City, N.Y.: Doubleday, 1975).

Thomas Howard, *Evangelical Is Not Enough* (Nashville: Thomas Nelson Publishers, 1984).

William A. Jurgens, *The Faith of the Early Fathers* (Collegeville, Minn.: Liturgical Press, 1970).

Pope John Paul II, *Crossing the Threshold of Hope* (Toronto: Alfred A. Knopf, 1994).

C. S. Lewis, *Miracles: A Preliminary Study* (New York: Macmillan, 1978).

————. *The Pilgrim's Regress* (Grand Rapids, Mich.: Eerdmans, 1992).

————. *The Problem of Pain* (New York: Macmillan, 1976).

————. *The Screwtape Letters* (New York: Macmillan, 1970).

————. *Surprised by Joy*, (New York: Harcourt Brace Jovanovich, 1955).

————. *The Weight of Glory* (New York: Macmillan, 1980).

Carl Olson and Sandra Miesel, *The Da Vinci Hoax* (San Francisco: Ignatius Press, 2003).

Ludwig Ott, *Fundamentals of Catholic Dogma* (Rockford, Ill.: TAN Books, 1974).

Jaroslav Pelikan, *Mary Through the Centuries: Her Place in the History of Culture* (New Haven, Conn.: Yale University Press, 1996).

Joseph Cardinal Ratzinger, *God and the World: A Conversation with Peter Seewald* (San Francisco: Ignatius Press, 2002).

Mark Shea and Dr. Ted Sri, *The Da Vinci Deception: 100 Questions About the Fact and Fiction of The Da Vinci Code* (West Chester, Pa.: Ascension Press, 2006).

Mark P. Shea, *By What Authority?: An Evangelical Discovers Catholic Tradition* (Huntington, Ind.: Our Sunday Visitor, 1996).

————. *Making Senses Out of Scripture: Reading the Bible as the First Christians Did* (Rancho Santa Fe, Calif.: Basilica, 1999).

————. *This Is My Body: An Evangelical Discovers the Real Presence* (Front Royal, Va.: Christendom, 1993).

Edward Sri, *Queen Mother: A Biblical Theology of Mary's Queenship* (Steubenville, Ohio: Emmaus Road, 2005).

Mark Twain, *Joan of Arc: Personal Recollections* (San Francisco: Ignatius Press, 1989).

George Weigel, *Witness to Hope: The Biography of Pope John Paul II* (New York: Harper Collins, 1999).

Ralph Woodrow, *The Babylon Connection?* (Riverside, Calif.: Ralph Woodrow Evangelistic Association, Inc., 1997).

Wright, David F., ed., *Chosen by God: Mary in Evangelical Perspective* (London: Marshall Pickering, 1989).

Online Resources

1913 *Catholic Encyclopedia*: http://oce.catholic.com.

Catechism of the Catholic Church: http://scborromeo.org/ccc.htm.

Catholic Answers' Mary and the Saints page: http://www.catholic.com/library/mary_saints.asp.

Ecumenical Society of the Blessed Virgin Mary: http://esbvm.org. A small group of Christians from several faith traditions who firmly believe that Mary may—just may—be a bridge to unity.

The Fathers of the Early Church: http://newadvent.org/fathers/.

Pope Pius IX, *Ineffabilis Deus:* http://newadvent.org/library /docs_pio9id.htm.

Pope Pius XII, *Munificentissimus Deus*: http://vatican.va/holy_fath er/pius_xii/apost_constitutions/documents/hf_p-xii_apc_195011 01_munificentissimus-deus_en.html.

Pope John Paul II, *Redemptor Hominis*: http://newadvent.org/library/docs_jpo2rh.htm.

———. *Redemptoris Mater*: http://newadvent.org/library/docs_jp o2rm.htm.

———. *Rosarium Virginis Mariae:* http://vatican.va/holy_father/john_paul_ii/apost_letters/documents/hf_jp-ii_apl_20021016_ros arium-virginis-mariae_en.html.

Theotokos Bookstore: http://www.theotokos.org.uk.

Index

This Index is for all three volumes of *Mary, Mother of the Son*. Roman numerals refer to volume and arabic numerals refer to page numbers.

About the Author

Mark P. Shea is author and co-author of numerous books, including the *New York Times* best-seller *A Guide to the Passion: 100 Questions About The Passion of the Christ* (Ascension Press), *By What Authority?: An Evangelical Discovers Catholic Tradition* (Our Sunday Visitor), *This is My Body: An Evangelical Discovers the Real Presence* (Christendom Press), *Making Senses Out of Scripture: Reading the Bible as the First Christians Did* (Basilica), and *The Da Vinci Deception: 100 Questions About the Fact and Fiction of The Da Vinci Code* (Ascension). An award-winning columnist, he contributes numerous articles to many magazines. In addition, Mark is Senior Content Editor for CatholicExchange.com and an internationally known speaker on the Catholic Faith. He can be found on line at http://www.markshea.blogspot.com or at http://www.mark-shea.com. He lives near Seattle with his wife, Janet, and their family.

About the Trilogy

Mary, Mother of the Son trilogy takes the reader on a *tour de force* exploration of the Marian dimension of Catholic thought, life, prayer, and practice.

In Volume One, *Modern Myths and Ancient Truth*, you discover the fascinating way in which Mary emerges with profundity, beauty, and love from the pages of Scripture in the light of apostolic teaching. You probe how the gospel of Christ crowns and perfects, not only the Old Testament, but the deepest insights of the great non-Christian philosophies, religions, and myths. You learn how to read the Bible as the earliest Christians did and find out how Mary safeguards the deepest truths about Christ and his Church.

In Volume Two, *First Guardian of the Faith*, you will learn about the biblical and apostolic roots of Mary's title as *Theotokos*; as well as her Perpetual Virginity, Immaculate Conception, and Assumption into heaven. In addition, you will discover the astonishing relevance each of these teachings has, not only for the Christian believer, but for the twenty-first century as it comes to grips with such questions as the dignity, origin, and destiny of the human person.

In Volume Three, *Miracles, Devotion, and Motherhood*, you will explore the devotional life of the Church: a life which includes not only the worship of the Father, Son, and Holy Spirit, but the communion of saints, the holy rosary, the mysteries of private revelation and Mary's God-given role as mother of all who believe in Christ.